Restructuring of International Economic Relations

Restructuring of International Economic Relations

Uruguay Round and the Developing Countries

SUMITRA CHISHTI

CONCEPT PUBLISHING COMPANY, NEW DELHI-110059

ISBN 81-7022-369-5

First Published 1991

Published and printed by
Ashok Kumar Mittal
Concept Publishing Company
A/15-16, Commercial Block, Mohan Garden
NEW DELHI-110059

Lasertypeset by
Microtech Advance Printing Systems (Pvt.) Ltd.
H-13, Bali Nagar
NEW DELHI-110015

To
my dear friend
SHEILA SANDHU

Contents

List of Tables

Introduction

The main determinant of the course, objectives and instruments of international economic relations is economic power. This power of a nation/region can stem from various sources: it may arise from the technological leadership; it may result from a high growth of industrial production and productivity relative to competitors; it can flow from the position of being a main/sole producer of strategic raw materials; and it can be the outcome of a large domestic market and huge financial resources. Of course, anyone of these advantages, supported by military power, would enable an endowed nation to act as a hegemonic state. The hegemony of such a single state has been the major factor in determining the course of international economic relations in the period after the Second World War. This is precisely what happened in the first two decades after the Second World War, when the United States of America, the hegemonic power, determined the course of international economic relations.

In the face of such power, new ideas, new approaches and new objectives can succeed only when the powerful nation/nations find it necessary and useful to support them. In the absence of any such support, the fate of new objectives and novel instruments is foredoomed. The attempts which are made to restructure economic relations without recognizing this fact may ultimately turn out to be a very frustrating exercise. Therefore, any endeavour to restructure international economic relations by any country or a group of countries should recognize the need to fulfill a necessary condition of possessing economic power.

During the colonial period, the international economic relations of developing countries were framed by the colonial powers consistent with their objectives and expectations. The tools and instruments they used were those which would benefit the executioner of these policies. The countries which became independent in the post-War period were quite conscious of this history. They were also aware of the inherent disadvantages that they suffered from when such policies were pursued by their colonial masters. Their national liberation movements had envisaged that once they became independent they would restructure their international economic relations in such a way as to meet their national needs. They hoped that the objectives of these relationships would change and the focus of interest would be their country/countries. Further , they also believed that through their presence as independent nations in the international comity of nations they would project their needs effectively. The inequities that they have inherited from the colonial past which had been extremely detrimental to their economic progress needed to be removed. They also made themselves believe that once they were politically independent, their options to negotiate with the international community for a new equitable international economic order would widen. This building up of the new international economic order was based not only on seeking justice for the exploited countries but also on invoking morality to do away with this injustice and the necessity of according the rightful place to a large section of humanity in the new economic order.

The attempts to restructure these relationships by the newly developing countries began in right earnest immediately after they won independence. Their first attempt was to dismantle the erstwhile structures and replace them with what they considered independent structures of their international relations. Soon, they realised that this task was not easy as they had believed it to be. The structures had deep roots in the economic and political powers that governed the international economic relations. These countries, therefore, steadily moved to adopt their policies with a limited confrontation with the powerful states.

The socialist countries of Eastern Europe and the Soviet Union endeavoured in this period to restructure their international economic relations on different principles. Hence we had the establishment of the Council of Mutual Economic Assistance (CMEA) which was expected to build a set of international economic relations based on the Marxit-Leninist ideology. Once the idea was accepted, attempts were made to pronounce new theories and concepts such as the theory of international socialist division of labour, CMEA price and integration of national plans. These countries faced a number of difficulties in structuring their integration on the basis of these principles. Hence they had to take recourse to various bilateral measures. More importantly, their relationships with the developed capitalist countries and developing countries which did not belong to the socialist system posed serious problems. Therefore, they found it useful to accept the principle of world price and international division of labour as the basis of international trade with the non-socialist countries.

These countries had stayed away from the international economic institutions. But they realised that it was important to participate in these organizations. Many of these countries sought the membership of the International Monetary Fund and the World Bank and became contracting parties of the General Agreement on Tariffs and Trade (GATT). There were, however, attempts in the GATT to modify the conditions under which they would participate.

These two groups, i.e., developing countries and (former) socialist countries of Eastern Europe, and the Soviet Union, also collaborated in the international forum with a view to bring about a new international economic order. They considered that their united endeavour would result in something concrete which would facilitate restructuring of international economic relations. No doubt these attempts led to the acceptance of some of the principles reluctantly by the powerful states. But, they could not build a strong edifice for a new international economic order because the powerful states did not participate in the process of building it. Their endeavour was either to prevent this restructuring taking place or to at least dilute its character. They have succeeded in their endeavour to a great extent.

The failure of a large number of developing countries to acquire the necessary economic strength to assert their way in the world economy made their attempts to restructure international economic relations more ineffective. Alongwith this, the collapse of the socialist system further weakened any attempt to restructure international economic relations in accordance with the perception of the developing countries.

The developing countries steadily lost their strength to pursue the objective of restructuring international economic relations as they perceived them. Their strength was reduced by a number of developments domestically and internationally, in the eighties. They were confronting a situation in which they needed to struggle to preserve their existing status.

They are thus on a crossroads at the beginning of the nineties. The approaches, concepts and strategies which they have hitherto adopted in a bid to improve the standard of life of their people on the one hand and enhance their status in the world economy, on the other, have lately met with unprecedented challenges, since their independence. These challenges have come not only from their failure to achieve the set goals but also due to the offensive launched by the developed countries to reorder the world economy solely consistent with their objectives and, if need be, to subjugate the interests of the developing countries explicitly to their own requirements. The multilateral trade negotiations launched in September 1986 at Punta del Este in Uruguay has finally formalised this offensive by the developed countries. The developing countries have been left with limited options. They are now compelled to reconsider their economic priorities nationally as well as globally not necessarily as they perceive but according to what is consistent with the global needs as defined by the developed countries.

The purpose of this book is to focus attention on this major problem as it has emanated from the Uruguay Round of Negotiations. This is a part of the author's larger study of restructuring of international economic institutions from the perspective of developing countries.

It is not claimed to cover here all the issues that have emerged in the Uruguay Round. Attention has been focussed only on some of the most vital issues of concern to developing countries and their consequent predicament.

I have drawn extensively on the help and cooperation of many colleagues and friends in this work. This needs specific mention for without their help I would not have ever completed this task. At the outset I would like to thank the Vice- Chancellor of Jawaharlal Nehru University, Professor M.S. Agwani, and the University. They enabled me to undertake the field work to Geneva and Washington to collect important material and to meet the eminent scholars in the field of study. I would also like to express my gratitude to Professor B.K. Shrivastava and Professor P.A.N. Murthy, former Deans, School of International Studies, JNU, and Professor Rahmatullah Khan, the present Dean, who helped me in conducting this study in various ways.

This study would not have been accomplished but for the most generous cooperation offered by Mr Hardeep Puri, Coordinator, MTN, UNCTAD, and Mrs Deepa Wadhwa, First Secretary, Indian Mission, Geneva. I express my indebtedness to them. I would like to record my grateful thanks to Mr. N.R. Rege, Director, Technical Barriers to Trade, the GATT, and Mr Ake Linden, Special Advisor to the Director-General of the GATT, who helped me in getting a proper insight into the intricacies of the subject.

April 1991 SUMITRA CHISHTI

1

Developing Countries in the World Economy in the Eighties

Following the Second World War the world witnessed the emergence of a large number of countries from their colonial status as independent countries which are now variously called 'developing' or 'third world' countries. Their political independence provided to them a source of confidence in their ability to forge independent economic relations with the world economy on the one hand and a collective strength to reconstruct the world economic system and relations consistent with their needs and aspirations on the other.

The initial enthusiasm of the developing countries can be attributed to a number of factors. The developed countries which had been the former metropolitan powers attempted to help these countries partly in their own self interest and partly as a gesture establishing their sense of enlightenment. This was reflected in their attempts to provide official development assistance and bilateral technical assistance. Their initiative was also accompanied by development of some multilateral institutions like World Bank and International Development Association (IDA) to provide concessional loans to the newly independent countries. This development was, however, contrary to the expectations of developing countries which had sought economic assistance programme channeled through the United Nations in which they have a majority in the decision-making set-up. The effective aid programmes have thus come to be promoted through bilateral channels as well as multilateral institutions in which the donor developed countries have kept their choices, preferences and objectives linked to their respective national interests. The multilateral aid programmes have been strictly monitored by specialised institutions like the World Bank with a weighted voting system in decision-making in which the developed countries have a decisive power to determine not only terms and conditions applicable to the lending policies of these institutions but also choice of the recipients of such aids. Nevertheless there had initially been considerable hesitation on the part of the developed countries to openly dictate terms which undermined national economic and political sovereignty of newly independent countries. Things, however, seem to be changing now.

Developing countries, having limited experience of adopting economic development strategies in the world economic environment with a large number of countries having achieved industrialization and a high level of economic development, believed in the availability of a number of options and alternatives for them to choose from. More importantly, there was little understanding of domestic political forces which would come to the fore once the economic benefits of growth started percolating unequally to various segments in their societies. This concealed problem made them expect exaggerated results from their endeavours.

Similarly, the developing countries had

unrealistic expectations from their unity in pursuing to establish a new international economic order consistent with their needs. This demand has been based on the power of bargain due to their collective strength. Here the developing countries have glossed over a number of fundamental issues which include the role of former metropolitan power in shaping their economic destiny, varying levels of development of developing countries which need different approaches and varying international problems of developing countries. They sought, in the early years, to establish a world economic order which would recognise their unequal strength and hence accord necessary positive discrimination to facilitate growth in addition to various supporting measures.

The existence of a vocal and supportive group of socialist countries led by the Soviet Union which aimed at helping the developing countries to achieve their objectives as part of its overall international strategy made these countries believe in the existence of an alternative path for economic development as well as an alternative paradigm of international economic relations from which the developing countries were expected to benefit.

Thus, in the three decades prior to the eighties, there had been a series of efforts by the developing countries and the international community to enable the former to achieve their objectives. A brief review of these developments is in order here. The developing countries endeavoured to establish a series of principles which enabled them to seek a favourable treatment in the execution of the internal economic programmes and also their importance in the world economy.

Attempts towards Restructuring the Trading System

In the fifties, attention was focussed most importantly on building into the world trading system a different approach to developing countries. While the establishment of International Trade Organization, which included in the scope of its functioning issues of direct relevance to economic development of developing countries, was aborted by the non-ratification of the agreement by the US Congress, the successor arrangement, General Agreement on Tariffs and Trade (GATT), had neither incorporated the special status of developing countries in the world economy nor focussed its attention on the problems of developing countries. Hence, in the fifties attempts were made to amend some of the Articles of the GATT. The most important amendment was effected by permitting the use of Quantitative Restrictions (QRs). Article XI which imposes a general prohibition on quantitative restrictions on imports, and Articles XII and XVIII that lay down the conditions under which QRs may be justified under the GATT. This was the result of the realization that a special need for QRs for developing countries to protect their balance of payments position existed. This recognition of the special need of the developing countries led to the introduction in 1957 of Article XVIII (Section B). The introduction of this Section implies that developing countries might need to take "protective or other measures affecting imports" in order to implement "programmes and policies of economic development designed to raise the general standard of living of their people". Thus, Article XVIII(B) was introduced whose provision was to apply only to developing countries with twofold objectives: first, to meet the needs arising from development efforts; and, secondly, to tackle problems arising from external instability as exhibited by instability in the prices of exports of these countries.[1]

This was followed by the introduction of Development Chapter (Chapter IV) in the GATT in 1965 which also reiterated the basic objective of raising the standard of living and progressive development of economies of contracting parties. It also recognized, in view of a wide gap between standards of living in less developed countries and developed countries, certain positive measures that needed to be taken. Developed countries were expected to accord a high priority to the reduction and elimination of barriers, not to introduce high tariffs and take all necessary measures towards these objectives.[2]

It is necessary to recognize right away that the introduction of Chapter IV as a part of the GATT Articles was in a way caused by the UN decision to establish the United Nations Conference on Trade and Development (UNCTAD). In 1962, the UN Conference on problems of developing countries in Cairo, attended by delegates of 36 States, led to the establishment of the UNCTAD which was expected to tackle the problems of trade and development of developing countries. The UNCTAD was established as a permanent organ of the General Assembly in spite of the reluctance of developed countries to the proposal for its formation. The UNCTAD was made directly responsible to the General Assembly rather than to the Economic and Social Council. The establishment of the UNCTAD also led to the acceptance of the principle of collective bargaining by the Group of 77 comprising developing countries which came into existence within the UNCTAD.[3] The UNCTAD-I (1964) enunciated a number of principles expected to govern world economic relations which were voted by a majority vote with the developed countries either voting against or abstaining.

For instance, general principle *four* enunciated that economic development and social progress should be the common concern of the whole international community ..." General principle *eight* stated that international trade should be conducted to mutual advantage on the basis of the most-favoured nation treatment and should be free from measures detrimental to the trading interests of other countries. However, the developed countries should grant concessions to all developing countries and extend to developing countries all concessions they grant to one another and should, in granting these or other concessions, require any concessions in return from developing countries. New preferential concessions, both tariff and non-tariff, should be made to developing countries as a whole and such preferences should not be extended to developed countries." General principle *six* states that international trade is one of the most important factors in economic development. "It should not be governed by such rules as are inconsistent with the attainment of economic and social progress and should not be hampered by measures incompatible therewith".

General principle *five* demands that national and international economic policies should be directed towards the attainment of an international division of labour in harmony with the needs and interests of developing countries in particular, and of the world as a whole. Developed countries should assist the developing countries in their efforts to speed up their economic and social progress, should cooperate in measures taken by developing countries for diversifying their economies and should encourage appropriate adjustments in their own economies to this end. The principles, numbering fifteen, have such expectations incorporated which, of course, are by and large, the demands of the developing countries.[4]

The basic principles of international trade relations, reciprocity and non-discrimination, as enunciated by the GATT, were being challenged all along by the developing countries in the UN and other fora in the fifties. This was also put across in multilateral trade negotiations under the GATT. They sought to build the principle of non-reciprocity in international trade negotiations. For the first time, this principle was accepted in the Kennedy Round of Trade Negotiations under which the developing countries were not expected to reciprocate equally for the tariff concessions that they received from the developed countries. The May 1963 Ministerial resolution had affirmed: "The developed countries cannot expect to receive reciprocity from the less developed countries."[5] Consequently, the developing countries which participated in the negotiations were not expected to offer reciprocal tariff concessions.

A more positive demand was expected to be achieved by the developing countries. They pursued this under the auspices of the UNCTAD. In the course of several years of negotiations an agreement on the principle of Generalised System of Preferences was reached in UNCTAD-II in 1968.

Generalized system of preferences which embodied preferential or free entry of manufactures and semi manufactures of developing countries into the markets of developed countries as adopted in the Resolution 21 (11) of UNCTAD 1968, was the result of a unanimous agreement among all the members of the UNCTAD. It involved a major change in the commercial policies as between developed market economy countries and the developing countries. It also embodied non-reciprocal, non-discriminatory system of preferences in favour of the developing countries. This was ofered by a 27 preference giving countries (See Appendix)

This pressure to accord a differential approach to the trade of developing countries and to make it an integral part of the GATT system continued. By its mandate on November 28, 1979, it was decided that notwithstanding the provision of Article 1 of the General Agreement (Most Favoured Nation Treatment to the contracting parties), the contracting parties were allowed to accord differential and more favourable treatment to developing countries without according such treatment to other contracting parties. A series of decisions were taken to enable contracting parties to accommodate this provision.[7]

It may be noted here that a number of these developments were actions which had been initiated after the declaration with regard to an International Economic Order by the UN. The Group of 77 decided to recommend to the UN General Assembly the need to declare the objective of establishment of a New International Economic Order with a view to remove the persistent severe economic imbalance in the relations between the developed and the developing countries and the consequent need for the mitigation of the current economic difficulties. To establish the New International Economic Order efforts were expected to be made for the establishment of sovereignty over natural resources, an integrated programme to stabilize the prices of primary products, establishment of a buffer stock, increased access of markets to the imports from the developing countries and promotion of cooperation among developing countries, control and regulation of transnational corporations, and increased transfer of resources including technology to developing countries. It was accompanied by the Charter of Economic Rights and Duties of States adopted by the XXIX Session of the UN which again aimed at increasing prosperity of developing countries to further strengthen the collective economic security of developing countries.[8]

Developing Countries in the International Monetary Fund and the World Bank

The developing countries also sought to take important steps to influence the working of the International Monetary Fund and the World Bank. In addition to their predominant voting power in these organizations, the developed countries (numbering 10) which met behind closed doors to discuss certain problems regarding the functioning of the international monetary system created a serious disquiet among the countries that were excluded as they felt that their views and interests were being disregarded. This, they felt, was contrary to the principle of international cooperation. The UNCTAD, and later G-24, representing the Group of 77, sought to participate fully in the complex international financial system by setting up compensatory mechanisms. In Lima, on November 7, 1971 the Ministerial Conference of the Group of 77 approved the 'Declaration and Principles of the Action Programme of Lima', a 13-point programme which expected to keep under review the course of the international monetary situation, evaluate monetary field as well as any decision which might be taken by a single country or a group of countries within the framework of the IMF relating to the interests of the developing countries and recommend to their governments on issues within the field of its competence to consider any other action. The Group was expected to function efficiently.[9]

On the transfer of resources including technology the developing countries endeavoured to press in the forum of the UN, especially in the UNCTAD, increased resource flow as a proportion of GNP of the developed countries. It was proposed in the UN in 1968 that developed countries must part with at least 0.70 per cent of their GNP to developing countries with no or limited conditions for official development assistance.

The terms and conditions of technology transfer were also studied in detail by experts in the UNCTAD with a view to help developing countries to enable them to buy technology cheaply. Also, they proposed a draft code for transfer of technology. This draft was completed in 1979.[10]

The developing countries were also deeply concerned about the role of Transnational Corporations (TNCs) and their challenge to the sovereignty of developing countries and their work which were often considered contrary to the needs of the economic development of developing countries. In a bid to enable the developing countries to control Transnational Corporations in their countries, in the mid-seventies they successfully made the UN establish under its aegis an organization, viz., Centre for Transnational Corporations, which was expected to perform two functions: *first*, to prepare a code of conduct to control the TNCs; and *second*, to help the developing countries to understand the complex working of TNCs and deal with them effectively. This Centre prepared a comprehensive code of conduct on TNCs which is still at the draft stage at it was in 1989.

Thus, till the end of the seventies, there were very slow but positive developments which were expected to redesign the relationship of developing countries in the world economy.[11] The eighties, however, witnessed that not only the continued efforts met with vigorous opposition from the developed countries, but also that serious attempts were being made consistently to reverse whatever small achievements were realized by the developing countries. The eighties can be considered as a lost decade for the developing countries in their search for a new international economic order to be established in the world economy. The optimists' belief that once the progress begins, it will be continuously kept up is not always true. Progress not only gets stopped very often, but also gets reversed which may take substantial time and effort to put back the wheels of progress and start to work once again. The developing countries in the world economy in the early years of the nineties are in a similar predicament of not only not progressing, but even losing whatever they had achieved, over the last three decades. One must hasten to add that the actual beneficial outcome of their achievements has remained a controversial subject which is not intended to be analysed here. It would suffice to say that there was a movement towards a 'friendly' world economic environment.

It is necessary to identify the factors which have given rise to this situation before analysing the types of developments which have a tremendous impact on their economies, their sovereignty and their status in the world economy. The discussion will be categorised into four main components: (i) Deteriorating position of developing countries in the world economy; (ii) Disarray among developing countries; (iii) Aggressive approach of developed countries, especially of the US, and (iv) Collapse of the Soviet influence.

Deterioration in the Economic Position of Developing Countries

The economic performance of developing countries in the eighties has been uneven not only over time but also between countries. The developing countries as a whole witnessed a deceleration of their economic growth.[12] The real GDP growth rate of all developing countries as estimated by the World Bank has been 5.9 per cent for the period 1965-80 while the growth experienced in the eighties was 4.3 per cent. This conceals the good performance of a few countries and inadequate performance of a large number of countries. Asia, and South Asia in fact, experienced higher growth rates in the eighties compared to the trend rate of the decade between 1965-80. The countries south of Sahara fared very badly during the period. A similar situation is noticed in the performance of per capita income growth. The developing countries in general experienced an actual decline in their per capita income growth rates while the sub-Saharan countries experienced a decline, the east Asian and south Asian countries experienced a decline in the ratio of their investment to the GDP. In fact, the eighties witnessed a steady decline in this ratio.

The international economic environment was not conducive to a sustained high growth rate. The expansion in exports of developing countries fell, as the world economic growth slowed, and imports of industrialised countries stagnated. In the mid-eighties, there has been a mild improvement. The share of developing countries in world exports steadily declined in the eighties as seen in Table 1.1.

TABLE 1.1: **Values of Exports**

in million US $
Shares are in the brackets

	1950	1960	1970	1975	1980	1985	1988
World	60,700	129,100	315,100	875,000	2,002,000	1,931,000	2,838,900
Developed Market	36,900	85,100	223,500	574,200	1,251,600	1,266,500	1,985,500
Economies	(60.8)	(65.9)	(70.9)	(65.6)	(62.5)	(65.6)	(69.9)
Developing countries	18,900	28,300	57,900	214,800	573,500	459,500	579,100
	(31.1)	(21.9)	(18.4)	(24.5)	(28.6)	(23.8)	(20.4)
Countries of Eastern	4,100	13,000	31,000	78,300	156,500	175,500	223,200
Europe	(3.0)	(4.3)	(4.1)	(3.8)	(3.8)	(4.5)	(3.9)
Socialist countries of	790	2,730	2,720	8,180	20,430	30,060	51,110
Asia	(1.3)	(2.1)	(0.9)	(0.9)	(1.0)	(1.6)	(1.8)

Source: UNCTAD, Handbook of *International Trade Statistics 1989, (UN, New York, 1990).*

The share of developing countries in world exports stood at 39.1 per cent in 1950 and declined to 20.4 per cent in 1988. The prices of primary products had fallen to an unprecedented level with limited hope of substantial improvement.[13]

In nominal terms, the non-oil commodity prices fell during the period 1982-1989 with a marginal improvement in 1988. The terms of trade of a large number of developing countries deteriorated with a reduction in their purchasing power. (Table 1.2) In 1985, the terms of trade index stood at 96 which was further reduced to 74 (base : 1980 = 100). Various estimates have been made to assess quantitatively the impact of this deterioration on developing countries. According to the UNCTAD, the resultant cumulative loss caused by terms of trade deterioration has been estimated to be $ 93 billion during the period 1981-86 for all developing countries.[14]

TABLE 1.2: **Terms of Trade of Developing Countries**

	Net Barter Terms of Trade	Purchasing Power indices of Exports
1980	100	100
1981	109	103
1982	104	92
1983	98	89
1984	98	94
1985	96	90
1986	71	82
1987	75	92
1988	71	100
1989	74	107

Source: UNCTAD, *Handbook of International Trade and Development Statistics*, 1989 (UN, New York, 1990) pp. 44-45.

The eighties also witnessed serious problems for

developing countries with regard to resources transfer. During the last three decades, the developing countries had enjoyed net transfer of resources. But since the middle of the eighties the developing countries experienced a reverse transfer of resources to developed countries. In some years of the late eighties, this accounted for 2 to 3 per cent of their GDP. In the year 1989, the developing countries as a group increased their net transfers to the rest of the world: to $42.9 billion from $37.6 billion in 1988.

The eighties witnessed a large growth in international debt of developing countries. Table 1.3 provides the growth of external debt of developing countries. In the case of severely indebted countries, the debt-GDP ratio stood at 50 per cent and debt-export ratio stood at 275 per cent, while in the case of moderately indebted countries, the debt-GDP ratio stood in the range of 30-50 per cent whereas the debt-export ratio reached the high figure of 165-275 per cent.

TABLE 1.3: **Growth of External Debt of Developing Countries (billion US dollars)**

	1982	1983	1984	1985	1986	1987	1988	1989
Total Debt of Develo-ping coun-tries	839	905	936	1041	1141	1292	1284	1290

Source: World Bank, *World Debt Tables.*

The financial flows to developing countries have declined in the eighties. The disbursement by the private creditors declined from $ 78.7 billion in 1980 to $ 44.4 billion in 1989 while the total disbursement declined from $ 100.4 billion in 1980 to $ 86.9 billion in 1989. The net flows also showed a marked decline. They declined from $ 62.7 billion in 1980 to $ 16.6 billion in 1989, the lowest level in the decade of eighties (Table 1.4). "The prospects for any increase in sources of external financing for the developing countries are not promising except for those involved in debt workout exercises and for countries implementing economic reforms. Reforming countries are better able to attract foreign investment and repatriated capital".[15]

While there has been growth in exports of manufactures by developing countries, they still constitute predominantly primary products based on a little processing. The protectionist measures of the developing countries persisted in the eighties. The tariffs on export products of interests to developing countries remained high despite tariffs reduction. For imports of developing countries, the non-tariff barriers increased. In addition, the initiatives under anti-dumping and countervailing measures have been more in the case of imports from developing countries than those from developed countries. During the period 1977-88, anti dumping investigations accounted for 77 per cent of all trade restrictions monitored by the GATT. Most of these are directed to imports from developing countries. The share of imports of developed countries from developing countries subject to non-tariff measures was less than 10 per cent in 1981 which increased to more than 20 per cent in 1986 while the imports from developed countries subject to these measures had been much less than 20 per cent. A significant feature of the world trade environment is the restriction of international trade in textiles. The Multi-Fibre Agreement (MFA) negotiated under the auspices of the GATT, between governments

TABLE 1.4: **Public and Private Long-Term Debt and Financial Flows, 1980-89 (billion US $) to Developing Countries**

Item	1980	1981	1982	1983	1984	1985	1986	1987	1988	1989
Debt disbursed and outstanding	427.9	496.1	560.8	643.8	685.8	781.3	884.4	1017.3	976.6	988.5
Disbursements	106.4	123.4	116.4	95.3	90.8	87.6	88.4	88.3	97.5	86.5
from private creditors	78.7	92.2	83.0	62.7	57.9	55.8	51.8	49.4	54.8	44.4
Debt Service	75.8	86.9	96.2	90.8	100.7	107.3	112.1	122.5	133.3	129.8
Principal	43.7	46.2	48.3	44.0	47.8	53.1	59.7	68.9	72.9	70.3
Interest	32.1	40.7	47.9	46.8	52.9	54.2	52.4	53.6	60.4	59.5
Net flows	62.7	77.2	68.1	51.3	43.0	34.5	28.7	19.4	22.8	16.6
Net transfers	30.6	36.5	20.2	4.5	-9.9	-19.7	-23.7	-34.2	-37.6	-42.9

Source: World Bank *Annual Report* 1990.

of importing and exporting countries of textiles has been a powerful arrangement to regulate trade in the products of great significance to developing countries.

While trade barriers such as tariffs and non-tariff measures were steadily reduced in the wake of multilateral trade negotiations, the 'grey area' measures, especially voluntary export controls, became an important mechanism through which world trade in a number of products have been managed. A large number of products of interest to developing countries either currently or prospectively have limited market access in developed countries consequent to these measures.

The developing countries also experienced an adverse impact of technology progress in developed countries. The technological improvements further reinforced the historical negative effects of decline in the use of raw materials in the industry. In fact, as Peter Drucker puts it, the technical progress uncoupled the relationship between industrial growth and the growth of demand for raw materials. The use of computer controlled machines and flexible manufacturing system reduced substantially the advantages of cheap labour that the developing countries possessed. Further, increased privatisation of technology has made the access to technology for developing countries more costly and difficult.[16]

Thus, many developing countries lost the gains made in the previous decades and emerged in the late eighties as more vulnerable than before to global forces in whose operation they have either little or no control.

Division Among Developing Countries

It must be stated that there has never been either unity among developing countries or uniformity in the levels of their economies and their economic interests. But there were four distinct binding forces among developing countries which enabled them to seek some common approach to their problems. *First,* while there was unevenness in the stages of economic development among them, it was not very pronounced. Since most of them had emerged from the colonial past, their level of economic development was not very divergent. *Second,* there was a perception that if the developing countries were to unite submerging their differences, the gains from this collective bargain will be more than in the case of individual approaches. *Third,* the developed countries were not totally opposed to this coming together of the developing countries. *Fourth,* the Socialist countries provided an alternative system and an alternative support to their endeavours. The losely united developing countries, however, could not bear the strains of the basic forces in the world economy which became prominent in the eighties.

Over the three decades, the economic performances of developing countries varied from country to country. Some of the developing countries emerged as newly industrializing countries while some are in the process of entering this group. Thus, the levels of economic development achieved by various developing countries differed substantially in the late seventies. It will not be wrong, therefore, to classify the resulting groups into three main categories: (a) newly industrializing countries with a high per capita income and relatively high ratio of industrial production to GDP; (b) emerging industrializing countries with a low per capita income but fast growing industrial production; and (c) the least developed countries with a low level of industrialization and a low level of per capita income. The details have been presented in Table 1.5.

These developments brought about a distinct shift in the need, perception and the policy approach towards the world economy by various developing countries. This obviously interfered substantially with the process of forging effective unity and cooperation among the developing countries.

The decade of the seventies had also witnessed a steady decline in the official development assistance. Hence, a large number of developing countries were compelled to seek alternative sources of finances. Inviting foreign direct investment became an important policy option that was available. Hence, a number of developing countries took recourse to various domestic and international policy measures to make them attractive for foreign direct investment. In this endeavour, there was also competition among some of the countries regarding the ways of making their economies most hospitable to foreign direct investment. Thus, a number of countries considered the importance of national policies whose objectives need not necessarily coincide with the group objective of developing countries. This included the approval of transnational corporations as well.

The IMF and the World Bank have been very active in financing the balance of payments needs as well as the development programmes of developing countries in the eighties. These financing measures have unhesitatingly and explicitly come under the conditionality linked with various lending programmes of these institutions. The IMF lending increased in the eighties. In 1980, the use of credit

TABLE 1.5: **Economic Indicators of Developing Countries**

	GDP Growth Rates		GNP per capita in 1988	Share of Industrial Production in percentage of GDP	
	1965-80	1980-88		1965-80	1980-88
Low Income Countries	5.4	6.4	$ 320	28	36
China and India	5.3	8.7	$ 340	32	40
Other Low Income Countries	5.5	2.0	$ 280	17	27
Middle Income Economies	6.1	2.9	$ 1930	33	40
Low Middle Income Economies	6.5	2.6	$ 1380	28	38
Upper Middle Income Countries	5.6	3.3	$ 3240	Average is not available For instance, South Korea 25	43

Source: World Bank, *World Development Report*, 1990.

by developing countries was only $ 12 billion which increased to $ 36 billion in 1990. Till 1985, there had been substantial increase in the amount committed by the IMF to developing countries which included lending under a number of new lending instruments. In 1980 the commitment was 10.8 billion SDRs which increased to 18.6 billion SDRs in 1984 and declined subsequently. But it shot up again to 13.9 billion SDRs in 1988.[17] The Sectoral Adjustment lending of the World Bank increased during the period 1979-80 from $ 31.5 million to $ 2283.5 million. It constituted only 0.3 per cent of the total lending in 1979 but the figure shot up to 14.0 per cent in 1986. Loans under Sectoral Adjustment lending have conditionality attached by the World Bank.[18] This further increased to $ 2534.6 million in 1990. Further, the World Bank also lends under Structural Adjustment programme with conditionality. In the year 1990 16 African countries availed of the facility under Structural Adjustment lending of the World Bank totalling $ 990 millions.[19] Many of them were the recipients of more than one Structural Adjustment loans. The conditionality has, in fact, prevented a large number of borrowing developing countries from pursuing economic policies other than what these donor institutions prescribe. The policy package under conditionality which is dominated by the free market philosophy has led many developing countries to pursue individual solutions rather than solutions based on a collective bargaining approach. Thus, at the beginning of the nineties a majority of the developing countries are beholden to the IMF and the World Bank for financial assistance and appear to be not interested in building up any collective self-reliance approach proclaimed by the Group of 77 in the seventies.

The late seventies and the eighties have been dominated by the resurgences of free market philosophy. This revival of a neo-classical approach to economy has forced many countries to reduce the importance of the state in managing the economy and the economic endeavour based on state initiative has been thoroughly discredited. Under the auspices of market economy approach the countries are expected to allow the functioning of global market forces without any intervention, in other words, following a neutral policy. All the developing countries are subscribing steadily to this view hoping that they would achieve economic efficiency on the one hand and necessary economic support for their efforts to improve their economies from the world economy on the other. Therefore, every country is for its own adjustment mechanism with the world economy rather than any collective approach.

The abandonment of socialism by the East European countries and the Soviet Union, their total acceptance of superiority of the market economy,[20] importance of foreign direct investment including transnationals and their changed approach to financial and technical assistance and trade to developing countries have left the developing countries with the possibility of not only drying up of this alternative aid and trade facility, but also an intellectual vacuum regarding the alternatives that could be devised to develop the economies consistent with their needs. This has made a large number of developing countries disillusioned about their previous national and international policies including their approach to cooperation among developing countries and its capacity to achieve the set objectives.

Cracks in the Group of 77 had begun to appear

early in the latc sixties and the seventies. The Organisation of Petroleum Exporting Countries (OPEC) increased the price of petroleum fourfold in 1973 by using the 'commodity power' enjoyed by the producers. A large number of developing countries were seriously affected by the rise. The efforts to have dual pricing for the developing countries and developed countries could not materialise. There was a disenchantment among the seriously affected developing countries about the use of 'commodity power' which would hurt not only developed economies but also developing countries dependent on petroleum import. This had led to a serious breach in the collective approach of the Group of 77. In fact, very often India was in this predicament. First, petroleum has been an important product of imports. The rise in its price had hit not only India's balance of payments, but also its domestic economy seriously. Second, it is also an important importer of a large number of non-ferrous metals while it is also an exporter of raw materials. In fact, India is a net importer of raw materials. For instance, a stabilisation programme of commodities initiated by the Group of 77 would create a dilemma for India of reconciling its national interest on the one hand and the strategy of the Group of 77 on the other.[21] While the break that could have come as a result of petroleum price hike somehow or the other was not made to surface very significantly, it is difficult to overlook its effect on the approach of a number of seriously affected developing countries.[22]

Even now, some of the important institutions designated to mould the approach of the countries of the South tend to believe in South as a unit with manageable differences — and they very often underestimate the factors that have grown over the years and are more divisive than cooperative. For instance, the report of the South Commission makes precisely the same mistake: "There must be no illusions regarding the enormity of the task of reversing the present unfavourable trends. International economic relations are, in the final analysis, power relations. Thus the countries that dominate the international economic system are unlikely to agree easily to reforms designed to redress the inequalities in the world distribution of income and wealth. Only a determined collective effort by the South could advance the prospect of meaningful North-South negotiations to restructure the present system of world economic relations".[23] While the Commission considers that the individual interests of developing countries and the pressure from the North tend to affect the solidarity of the South, it puts the incapacity to negotiate on the part of the South as an equal factor arising from the failure to achieve collective bargaining. The South, therefore, has not yet come up to grapple with the fundamental problems which are leading to its increasing fragmentation.

Changed Approach of Developed Countries towards Developing Countries in the Eighties

There has been a systematic endeavour to establish bilateral and regional relationships with the developing countries by the former metropolitan powers and the US. The South Commission has also recognized this. As it put it in the context of the Uruguay Round: "Developing countries share fundamental common interests and positions on the broad framework of the Uruguay Round. At the same time, developing countries as a large group have different interests in relation to many of the specific issues under negotiation in the Round.

Developed countries were not slow in recognizing these potential divergences, and their possible disrupting impact on the common political stand of the G-77 countries in the negotiations. Indeed, the emphasis on the heterogeneity of the South's interests has underlined all the moves by developed countries towards 'graduation' of the relatively more advanced developing countries and not only in relation to the GATT".[24] When the European Economic Community came into existence in 1950, it forged special relations with a number of African countries which were the former colonies of France and other members of EEC. These relationships included preferential treatment for the exports of their former colonies in EEC markets, reverse of preference for exports of EEC in these markets, a fund for stabilising export earnings of these countries — Stabex and various other measures. This had always been an important factor in the approach of a number of African countries towards the policy of the Group of 77. This preferential cooperation between the EEC and other African and Pacific countries is continuing under the Lome Convention which has been periodically signed by 43 ACP developing countries. This has always been a source of divergence of interest among the developing countries.

The US has endeavoured to foster closer relationships with the Latin American countries. Many of the Latin American countries depend to a large extent on the US markets for their exports. The transnationals of the US play an important role in these countries, thus preventing any major initiative of cooperation among developing countries becoming successful. Further, the serious international debt crisis of a large number of Latin American countries made them more vulnerable to pressures of the US and multilateral financial institutions dominated by the US. The Baker and Brady plans for debt relief which have been primarily designed to help these countries further reinforced the necessity for these countries to pursue policies which are not in basic contradiction with the policy dictates of the US.

The eighties witnessed a radical shift in the political and economic environment in the world. The developed countries, especially the US and the UK, were led by the leaders who subscribed to the theory of supremacy of the market forces in the economies and reduction of government's role in the economic management. Steadily, the welfare state got dismantled and replaced by a state which pursued macro economic policies which enabled the market forces to function efficiently. In fact, the efficiency consideration became the dominant objective of the economies and the government policies. Further, what was perceived to be good domestically was considered to be good internationally. The consequence of this on the North- South relations or the relations among the developing countries was, in fact, very significant.

The developed countries' governments in a bid to reduce the state's role have increasingly argued that the developing countries should depend more on private flows of capital.[25] Hence, they have begun pressurizing the developing countries to alter their domestic policies in such a way that they would become attractive to foreign direct investment and the operation of transnational corporations.

Further, the developed countries have become keenly interested in the growing economies of developing countries for their exports not only of merchandise but also services. As a result, they would like the developing countries to open up their markets. In this endeavour they have pursued bilateral and unilateral approaches. The US has earned the distinction of using these new methods to seek what is known as 'crow bar technique' to open up the market under Clauses Special 301 and Super 301 of the American Omnibus Trade and Competitiveness Act 1988. Consequently, the developing countries have opened their markets substantially.[26]

The developed countries have also become concerned about the growth of exports of industrial products from developing countries. Imports by the US of manufactures from developing countries increased by 17 per cent per year in nominal terms in the first eight years of the decade reaching $ 122,000 million in 1988, almost a fourfold rise from 1980. The European Community imported $ 90,000 million worth of manufactures in 1988, while the figure was only $ 40,000 million in 1980. Japan also imported worth $ 80,000 million in 1980 which increased to $ 830,000 million in 1988.[27]

These exports have touched off various domestic lobbies to force their governments to intervene in a number of ways. Apart from taking recourse to protectionism, the developed countries have begun attacking some of the advantages that the developing countries had achieved during the last three decades. The various areas under threat will be discussed subsequently. They include continuation of special and differential treatment, non-reciprocity, liberty to pursue policies with regard to technology, alleged counterfeiting of trade and performance criteria for foreign direct investment etc. These have affected the course of international economic relations between developed and developing countries.

NOTES

1. The working party on Quantitative Restrictions established in the GATT felt "the contracting parties recognize further that it may be necessary for those contracting parties, in order to implement programmes and policies of economic development designed to raise the general standard of living of their people, to take protective or other measures affecting imports, and that such measures are justified in so far as they facilitate attainment of the objectives of this agreement..." Paper presented by the GATT Secretariat, (Mimeographed) and also see for an excellent discussion of the subject, Frances Stewart, 'Proposals for a Review of GATT Article XVIII: An Assessment', in UN, *Uruguay Round Papers on Selected Issues* (UN, 1989), pp. 1-31.
2. GATT Articles and Part IV of the GATT.
3. See for detailed discussion. Robert F. Meagher, *An International Redistribution of Wealth and Power: A study of the charter of Economic Rights and Duties* of States (Oxford and IBH Publishing Company, Calcutta, 1979).
4. See for details, UN, *Proceedings of the United Nations Conference on Trade and Development: Final Act and Report* (New York, 1964), pp. 10-30.
5. Government of India, *Kennedy Round of Trade Negotiations* (New Delhi, 1965).
6. Indian Institute of Foreign Trade, *UNCTAD-II* (Indian Institute of Foreign Trade, New Delhi, 1968). Graig R. Macphee, 'A Synthesis of the GSP Study Programme,' *Foreign Trade Review*, Vol. XXIV, No. 2, July-September 1989.
7. GATT, *Differential and More Favourable Treatment, Reciprocity and Fuller Participation of Developing Countries*, Decision of 28 November 1979 (L 4903).
8. Programme of Action on the Establishment of a New International Economic Order, UN Resolution No. 3201 (S-VI) May 1974, Charter of Economic Rights and Duties of States. Resolution of General Assembly 3281, December 1974.
9. Intergovernmental Group of Twenty Four on International Monetary Affairs, *Documents of the G-24* (Mimeographed).

10. UNCTAD, *Draft Code of Transfer of Technology* (Various Reports).
11. Some experts have argued that these developments did not result in restructuring international economic relations. They were just reforms in the system. See Robert F. Meagher, *An International Redistribution*, pp. 129-44.
12. *World Development Report*, 1990.
13. *Ibid*
14. See for details, Sumitra Chishti, 'Crisis in International Economic Cooperation and the Economic Development of Third World Countries', *International Studies*, Vol. 26, 2, 1989. World Bank, 'Price Prospects for Major Primary Products', *World Bank News*, Vol. X, No. 9.
15. World Bank Annual Report, 1990, pp. 31-32.
16. Peter Drucker, 'The Changed World Economy', *Foreign Affairs*, Spring 1986 and Sumitra Chishti, 'Crisis in International Cooperation'. Also see, Man Mohan Singh, 'Development Policy Research: The Tasks Ahead'. Keynote Address, *Annual Conference on Development Economics*, 1989.
17. World Bank, *World Debt Tables*, 1990-91 IMF, *Annual Report*, 1990, p. 71.
18. World Bank, *Annual Report*, 1986, p. 47.
19. World Bank, *Annual Report*, 1990, p. 55.
20. See Sumitra Chishti,, 'Reforms in the Centrally Planned Developed Economies and their Impact on Trade and Economic Relations with the Non-Centrally Planned Developing Economies', UN *Journal of Development Planning*, No. 20, 1990.
21. Sumitra Chishti, 'World Economic Environment, Developing Countries and the New Round of Multilateral Trade Negotiations', *Foreign Trade Review*, Vol. XX, 1985, pp. 110-115.
22. The difficulties arose is convening the first Conference on International Economic Cooperation (first Preparatory Meeting April 1975) in Paris. While the US was creating problems, some developing countries were anxious to resolve the difficulties that they faced after the oil price hike. See for discussion Meager, *An International Redistribution of Wealth and Power*, pp 92-95.

23. *The Challenge to the South, Report of the South Commission* (Oxford University Press, Oxford, 1990), pp. 20-21.
24. South Commission, *Statement on the Uruguay Round,* (South Commission, Adopted at its Third Meeting, Mexico, 5-8 August 1988), p. 7.
25. See for detailed discussion, Indian Institute of Foreign Trade, *Foreign Direct Investment in India, Malaysia and South Korea* (Mimeographed). UNCTC, *Transnational Corporations in World Development: Trends and Prospects* (UN, New York, 1988). Sumitra Chishti and Anees Chishti, *Transnationals and Developing Countries* (Allied Publishers Ltd., New Delhi, 1990).
26. See for an excellent discussion of US trade policy and its imperatives, Jagdish N. Bhagwati, 'United States Trade Policy at Cross Roads', *Journal of World Economy,* January 1990.
27. This has been a subject matter of debate even in the 70s. A number of studies on imports of newly industrializing countries were made by the OECD. These figures are drawn from the study of International Finance, *Exporting to Industrial Countries* (IFC, 1990).

2

Challenges to the Developing Countries under the Uruguay Round of Multilateral Trade Negotiations

The eighties not only witnessed a steady growth in the efforts of developed countries to dismantle the arrangements made in the world trading system to enable the developing countries to participate in it effectively, but also saw the birth of new issues, concepts and approaches the impact of which on economies, trade and finance of developing countries is uncertain.

The late seventies and the early eighties saw the collapse of the consensus on approaches to economic development of developing countries. The approaches that dominated the development efforts in the sixties and the seventies were no longer accepted. On the other hand, new approaches and new theories determined the course of the development efforts. *First*, the import substitution approach was thought to result in inadequate growth and inefficiency. Hence, it was argued that export-led growth was a strategy superior to the one of import substitution.[1] According to this understanding the relatively higher growth rates enjoyed by a few countries with large exports were considered as evidence to the growth potential of this strategy. Hence, it is argued that a policy mix promoting export-led industrialisation must be encouraged. *Second*, the state-led industrialisation accompanied by the growth of public sector was deemed to be highly inefficient, and incapable of accelerating the economic growth in developing countries. *Third*, the basic approaches to international support for the State's development effort were also not considered conducive to growth. *Fourth*, it gave rise to the furthering of the development strategy based on an effective functioning of international market forces and increased participation in the world economy which would result in a more efficient and enduring economic development than in cases of other strategies. Thus the international economic structures created by the approach of positive intervention by the state were to a large extent dismantled.

This shift in the approach to economic development strategies and the propagation of an efficient use of market forces led not only to abandon hitherto followed economic development strategies of developing countries, but also encouraged the efforts to dismantle the international policy structure which was developed over the last three decades had in them the extension of the elements of theories and approaches that governed development effort of developing countries over the last decade.

The assault came in marginalising the role of UNCTAD. The history of UNCTAD-III, UNCTAD-IV, UNCTAD-V, UNCTAD-VI and UNCTAD-VII shows that these conferences were unable to achieve any important objectives set out in the agenda and final conclusions. The UNCTAD-VII which met in 1987 was convened with great amount of difficulty and in fact questions were raised whether UNCTAD-VII should be held at all. Further, very few countries wanted to host the conference. Cuba wanted to host it, but such a proposal was not accepted by the US. Thus it was convened in Geneva. The agenda setting was once again made a difficult task.[2] The conclusions of the conference were also insignificant. "The negotiating process during the Conference was marked by a non-confrontational atmosphere. The earlier stand of some countries that the role of UNCTAD should be limited to analysis of issues and exchange of views was not pursued beyond a point and soon after the conference started the regional groups got in the process of detailed negotiations on specific elements with the objective of arriving at concrete results by consensus. However, despite the constructive dialogue in the early stages, by the end of third week, the negotiations on specific policies and measures remained deadlocked, notably in the area of debt and international trade". The Final Act of UNCTAD-VII was adopted by consensus.[3] But no specific action was to be implemented seriously.

Thus, the eighties witnessed the steady erosion of an institution under the aegis of the UN which could not carry on its assigned mandate because the important members could not provide the necessary support to its functioning. It was feared that the UNCTAD would be wound up. With a bit of persuasion the institution in its skeletal form is continuing with marginal importance. The reason to lament this state of affairs is that in the sixties and seventies, the developing countries had placed their faith in making the UNCTAD an instrument for establishing a new international economic order through collective bargaining.

The measure of UNCTAD's ineffectiveness is that a number of causes that it espoused in the seventies such as an Integrated Programme of Commodities, establishment of Common Fund, etc., no longer figure as important items of its agenda. In fact, the Common Fund was established in July 1989 in which the role of the UNCTAD has been minimal.[4]

The disenchantment of developing countries with the UNCTAD can be seen in the increasing number of developing countries becoming the contracting parties of the GATT. In fact, a large number of developing countries did not join the GATT, treating it as 'a rich man's club' and sought to find solutions to their trade problems through the UN, i.e., the UNCTAD. As in 1989, the total number of contracting parties of the GATT increased from 23 initially to 97 of which 25 are industrial countries (EC member states: 12), 9 advanced developing countries, 57 developing countries and six non-market economies.

Multilateral Trade Negotiations

The post-war world witnessed a serious attempt on the part of developed countries to dismantle trade barriers erected during the inter-war period, especially the tariff walls. The most important success of the GATT since 1947 has been the reduction of tariff levels among the contracting parties. This happened as a result of seven intensive negotiating rounds, beginning in general in 1947. Table 2.1 gives the series of rounds.

While all other rounds aimed at reducing tariffs, the sixth, the Kennedy Round, planned to look seriously at non-tariff barriers, but that aim was only minimally achieved. The Tokyo Round in 1970s was the first major negotiating round held to make non-tariff barriers a priority objective of the negotiations.

TABLE 2.1: **GATT Negotiating Rounds**

Round	Dates	No. of countries	Value of Trade covered
Geneva	1947	23	$ 10 billion
Annecy	1949	33	Unavailable
Torquay	1950	34	Unavailable
Geneva	1956	22	$ 2.5 billion
Dillion	1961-1	45	$ 4.9 billion
Kennedy	1962-7	48	$ 40 billion
Tokyo	1973-9	99	$ 155 billion
Uruguay	1986	107	—

Source: John H. Jackson, *Restructuring the GATT System*, (Royal Institute of International Affairs, Pinters Publishers, London, 1990), p. 37. GATT. *Focus*, October, 1986.

After the completion of the Tokyo Round in 1979, it became obvious that a new round was necessary. It is partly attributed to bicycle theory of trade policy implying that unless there is a forward movement, the bicycle will fall over. If there were no initiatives on trade policy, the temptations of national governments to backslide would be very great. Further, a large number of developments in the world economy had made it more complex and interdependent. A number of subjects required attention. It was considered that the GATT with its original mandate was not in a position to tackle problems created by these developments. A fresh mandate was required.[5] It also included a number of controversial subjects from the point of view of developing countries such as liberalisation of international trade in services, trade related intellectual property rights and trade related investment measures. A meeting was held at Punta del Este (Uruguay) during September 15-20, 1986 on the occasion of the special session of the GATT contracting parties. Ministers of the GATT member countries adopted at this meeting a declaration launching a new round of multilateral trade negotiations. It has two parts. Part I of the declaration deals with trade in goods. Part II deals with launching of negotiations on trade in services. It consisted of 107 countries; 97 contracting parties and 10 non-contracting parties. In all fifteen subject areas have been covered for negotiations: tariffs, non-tariff barriers, agriculture, textiles, tropical products, anti-dumping and countervailing measures, safeguards, future of the GATT system, trade related aspects of investment measures, services, GATT Articles, dispute settlement and subsidies.

Developing Countries and the Uruguay Round of Trade Negotiations

The Uruguay Round of Trade Negotiations, unlike the previous rounds, not only included a large number of subject areas which were not tradc (merchandise) related aspects, it also brought under its coverage a re-examination of principles, articles and provisions in the GATT which had been included to facilitate effective participation of developing countries in the world trading system and promote their economic devclopment.

Provision on Balance of Payments and Developing Countries in the GATT

Under the GATT system, the developing countries have been permitted under Article XVIII B to use quantitative restrictions on imports to correct their balance of payments as has already been discussed. The developed countries led by the US have mounted an attack on this facility enjoyed by the developing countries in the Uruguay Round.

The United States believes that many developing countries have misused these provisions by restricting imports in the specific sectors rather than across the board and by continuing the use of such restrictions even after balance of payments (BOP) situation has been stabilised. Further, it is argued that trade restrictions are harmful to world economic growth and development and are the least efficient means of dealing with BOP difficulties. World economy has undergone major changes. These changes no longer justify Section B of Article XVIII. It is also argued by the US that the developing countries, with this power, will have the capability to negate the effects of their trade liberalisation by the unfettered use of the relevant provisions. The developing countries have opposed the approach of eliminating this facility.

In an effort to shift the developing countries' reliance on Article XVIII B, the US and Canada proposed in December 1989 in Uruguay Round Negotiations an alternative proposition in which the US wanted to provide guidelines for taking limited kinds of actions that countries facing serious BOP problems were entitled to take and to strengthen disciplines and procedures which apply to countries wishing to take measures in excess of those specified in the guidelines. The European Community also tabled a similar paper which was subsequently merged with the US/Canada/EEC paper. The developing countries were united and opposed any discussion of this provision. However, the US and other developed countries asserted that the developing countries should be prepared to negotiate on this issue if they expected the developed countries to make concessions in areas of interest to them. In a subsequent proposal the developed countries have argued that if there is a necessity of introducing restrictions for balance of payments reasons, it is expected that the Balance of Payments Committee of the GATT should play a more active role. For such exceptional BOP measures, the balance of rights and obligations between invoking countries and their trading partners should be decided by the members of the GATT rather than by automatically applied rules. The negotiating group on balance of payments discussed it in detail. But it has not been possible to reach an agreement. As in December 1990, the Draft Final Act of Uruguay Round states: "It has not yet been decided whether or not to engage a negotiation on the subject".[6] While a temporary reprieve has been achieved by the developing countries, it is difficult to expect that this facility will continue to be unquestioned in the coming years. Further, if a new organisational structure such as a Multilateral Trade Organisation comes into effect in the coming years, as proposed, the fate of such facilities is uncertain. The draft proposals do not provide for any different principles governing the trade of developing countries.

The Principle of Non-Discrimination and the Most Favoured Nations Treatment (MFN) under the GATT System, Reciprocity and Free Rider Problem

The developing countries, as has been noticed, have been exempted from offering reciprocal concessions in multilateral trade negotiations under the auspices of the GATT. This has not been appreciated by the developed countries, especially the US.

The principle of non-discrimination in international trade is widely recognised as being the best, possibly the only, basis upon which sound international trade relations can be built which can construct a stable international economic order. It is expected that it would reward the efficiency while violating the principle of non-discrimination would snowball into discriminatory policies. The non-discrimination principle is enshrined in Most Favoured Nations Treatment of traded goods, that is, all imported goods, to receive the same tariff or non-tariff treatment irrespective of their country of origin, and national treatment, that is, imported goods and national goods to receive the same treatment once the former have paid their customs duties.

Historically, the countries began using the MFN principle in the nineteenth century. All international trade treaty arrangements had MFN clauses. This clause took new forms : unconditional and conditional. The unconditional form obligated a treaty signatory to extend to its co-signatory any trade concessions granted to third countries now or in the future without reservation. The conditional MFN clause granted the co-signatory opportunity to enjoy the same treatment as third country provided it offered the same compensation as the other country had given to obtain a favoured treatment. The most important practitioner of conditional MFN had been the US. Until 1923, the US maintained that MFN pledges must be interpreted as conditional even when precise words of treaty are unclear.[7]

The inter-War period witnessed the collapse of all trading principles. Discrimination, restrictions, bilateralism and various controls dominated the international trade scene which fragmented the world economy. This experience influenced the negotiators of the GATT to emphasise on a liberal non-discriminatory trading system which is unconditional. Thus, Article 1 of the GATT required that:

"... any advantage, favour, privilege of immunity granted by any contracting party to any product originating in or destined for any other country shall be accorded immediately and unconditionally to the like product originating or destined for the territory of all other contracting parties". Thus, the cornerstone of the GATT is extension of unconditional most-favoured nation treatment to all fellow signatories.

It must be stated that despite this commitment to unconditional MFN treatment, the GATT did not exclude all discriminatory trade policies. It had provided a number of exceptions, for instance, the inclusion of a grandfather clause permitting continued application of existing preferential trade arrangements (Article 1, para 2). The most significant exception to the MFN treatment set out in the GATT is contained in Article XXIV which states conditions under which GATT signatories may form economic unions and free trade areas. The three main conditions are:

(i) trade barriers facing non-members must not, on the whole, be higher than those previously in effect;
(ii) trade barriers must be eliminated on "substantially all" trade among members; and
(iii) interim arrangements to permit forming of customs union or free trade area must be completed over a reasonable period of time.[8]

It has been very often argued that the MFN treatment under the GATT system along with the concessions to developing countries not requiring them to reciprocate has made them enjoy the benefits of trade liberalisation without any costs entailed in reciprocity. Hence, it is now argued that developing countries must pay costs through offering some reciprocal concessions. This demand finally found expression in the code system in the Tokyo Round of Negotiations. One commentator of the GATT puts it thus : "The attraction of code approach grew in proportion to developed country irritation with developing country interventions in every day GATT business. By the late 1960s, such irritation was much in evidence. It had become difficult to consider any subject in GATT meetings without finding developing countries insisting forcefully on some special measure for their own benefit. Developing countries viewed this continuing nagging as a tactic fully justified by their urgent economic needs. They were prepared to bloc action anywhere, until attention was given to those needs. Unfortunately, the nagging often seemed more ceremony than substance because developed countries were usually unwilling or unable to do anything meaningful. In those cases, the developing countries would often consume a great deal of time to obtain nothing more than few additional words in a document pledging for the hundredth time that developing country needs would be taken into account".[9]

The nine agreements signed on various non-tariff barriers, subsidies, etc. for the first time, are draped as "stand alone" treaties each with signatory clauses, and in most cases with institutional measures which amounted to balkanisation of the GATT system. Some of these agreements seek waivers from other GATT obligations. "As stand alone treaties, the codes bind only those nations which sign and ratify them". This has led to a number of questions. In theory GATT parties which do not sign the agreements are not bound by them and no provision of a code can alter their GATT rights. This was agreed upon at the time of the 1979 decision.

The developed countries' reluctance to accept special treatment to all developing countries was expressed in yet another way. In the Tokyo Round this unhappiness was expressed in promoting the concept of 'graduation' to accord non-reciprocal treatment to developing countries. In fact one of the most serious problems in the Ministerial meeting in Tokyo Round was the issue of graduation. Under this the developed among the developing countries were expected to offer reciprocal concessions. "One important issue concerned the least developed countries and the extent to which special treatment being accorded to other developing countries".[10] This was introduced in a specific form as will be seen later.

In practice, two problems have arisen with the codes. One, that they were drawn up among a few countries which excluded participation of others in deciding upon key aspects of the substantive rules. This process had a profoundly alienating effect on the excluded countries and raised serious doubts about whether provisions under various codes reflected their national interests. The other problem is that codes carry the potential of being applied in a discriminatory or damaging way against non-signatories. Although this has not been the case in practice, with the exception of one or two codes, the potential is certainly there and the clearest system for doing so would be to extract reciprocity and eliminate free riding.[11]

The Punta Del Este declaration launching the Uruguay Round states that "the developed countries do not expect reciprocity for commitment made by them in trade negotiations to reduce or remove tariffs and other barriers to trade of developing countries in the course of trade negotiations, to make contributions which are inconsistent with their individual development, financial and trade needs".[12] Yet the negotiations in the Uruguay Round have underlined one fact that the developing countries must reciprocate. In fact, trade liberalisation in the developing countries has already begun under various pressures although they are not strictly related to the Uruguay Round. They include conditionality associated with structural adjustment lending by the IMF and the World Bank and unilateral demands from the US made under its various Trade Act provisions to open the markets and provide non-discriminatory access to markets and finally the desire on the part of a number of developing countries to invite foreign direct investment by providing policy incentives of which trade liberalisation is one. In fact, even countries like India have offered to reduce tariffs by 30 per cent in the Uruguay Round.

In this context, it is necessary to examine the issue of reciprocity and free rider's problem in a greater detail. Two perceptive observers have pointed out: "In the days when the GATT had only 23 member countries which all took an active interest in its deliberations, there was no contradiction between MFN treatment and reciprocity. In GATT rounds of multilateral trade negotiations, a series of bilateral bargaining was struck between contracting parties, then 'multilateralised' via MFN principle to all member countries of the system. All contributed to the outcome. All received benefits. But even then one could see that a 'free rider' problem might emerge sometime in the future: that a member of the GATT could sit on the fence, collect all the benefits of MFN tariff reductions, while offering little or nothing to its partners in exchange. Unless a policeman is there to enforce reciprocity one of the two principles have to be sacrificed".[13]

It is argued that MFN with non-reciprocity has perpetuated a system of privileges of the world trading system where a large number of beneficiaries of these privileges do not offer any kind of return to enjoy these privileges. In other words there are no reciprocal concessions/facilities offered by these 'free riders'. It may be noticed that most of the developing countries are treated as free riders. It is further considered that by enjoying certain additional privileges under Generalised System of Preferences, these developing countries have been enjoying, as one expert on GATT has observed, "over the years the relationship (between developed and developing countries) has gravitated, in seemingly inexorable fashion, towards the one-sided welfare relationship demanded by the developing countries".[14]

In the view of the present author the free rider advantage and its benefits to the recipient countries under the prevailing system are exaggerated thus leading to wrong conclusions in international trade and economic policies.

(a) Under the Kennedy Round as well as the Tokyo Round of Multilateral Trade Negotiations where reciprocity has not been enforced on developing countries, the bulk of tariff concessions were exchanged among the developed countries on products of interest to developed countries. The developing countries were least benefited on account of this: (i) Many of the primary products, the major exports of developing countries, were already duty free or had lower rates of duty; (ii) reductions resulting from Multilateral Trade Negotiations were deeper on manufactures than on semi-manufactures; (iii) when products of future export interest to developing countries were taken into consideration, only the tariff benefits became recognisable; a GATT study observes: "As for tariffs facing exports of developing countries, the average in a Multilateral Trade Negotiations reduction on industrial products was less deep than the overall cut, about one quarter compared with one third. This reflects the fact that the products to which the tariff-cutting formula was not applied are relatively more important in exports from developing countries".[15] The agricultural trade has largely remained untouched by the GATT rules so far.

(b) While the participant developing countries were not expected to accord reciprocity, nineteen developing countries offered tariff reductions or bindings of prevailing tariff rates under the Tokyo Round for developed countries insisted on at least a token reduction.

(c) The much publicised Generalised System of Preferences has a number of limitations which have substantially restricted the accrual of benefits in any significant manner to the developing countries' exports. *First*, a large number of products of interest to developing countries are under ceilings, quotas or exceptions: these include textiles, shoes, steel and some manufactures. *Second*, some important agricultural products are not eligible for concessions. *Third*, the GSP is a temporary arrangement which has been offered for a certain period, that is being extended periodically without any assurance of its continuance while there is a possible threat of withdrawal if a donor considers the recipient is not behaving as expected not only in trade matters but also in other economic matters. *Fourth*, those countries which become competitive immediately lose this facility as it happened in the case of South Korea and Taiwan. They have been removed from the list of countries accorded a beneficiary status under the Generalised System of Preferences as the US saying that they had attained competitiveness.[16] *Fifth*, the reduction of tariffs following Multilateral Trade Negotiations would increasingly reduce the advantages that the developing countries enjoyed in a number of products. And, *finally*, many exports are being made by the transnational corporations taking the advantagc of GSP which has facilitated gains to donor countries, i.e., home countries of these TNCs significantly by the offshore production of TNCs of the US.

Thus it can be seen that the free rider is not really a free rider. He docs not have all things on which he can take a free ride. Secondly, when he has these things, he is not given an opportunity to do so. Even the normal regulations were altered to disable him in riding effectively. The MFA regulating international trade in textiles is a shining example of this predicament of developing countries.

There is an argument that developing countries have enjoyed the benefits of non-reciprocity for a substantial period of time and hence it is time now to demand from them the dismantling of their defences. This argument is untenable judged from the historical experience of currently developed countries which are demanding this and their current behaviour with regard to certain sectors of trade where the developing countries are efficient producers.

Further, import restriction of developing countries did not actually result in contraction of their imports. In fact, the growing imbalance in the international trade of a large number of developing countries is the proof that they have increased imports despite the restrictions.

It is argued by some that reciprocity or utility is in the eye of the beholder. It is further stated that reciprocity cannot be defined.[17] If the beholder is a hegemon like the US, then it is indeed a difficult world for the concept of reciprocity would be defined by the way the US understands it. This is precisely what is happening.

It is important to understand new concepts of reciprocity which are increasingly governing the approaches of developed countries especially the United States. The policy as stated by the US is the most clear and unambiguous understanding. This has been clearly indicated in US-Canada Free Trade Agreement of 1988, which was preceded by the Free Trade Agreement with Israel. These two agreements heralded the departure of the US from its own conscious policy of not exploiting the GATT's Article XXIV which provides for departures from the principles of non-discrimination to form free trade areas or custom unions. Another indicator to this effect has been the passage by the US Congress of the Omnibus Trade and Competitiveness Act of 1988. Section 301 of the Trade Act of 1974 has been hitherto applied as a remedy for treaty-defined unfair trade practices determined as such under multilateral procedures when the GATT obligations were in question. Section 301 under the new Act has been turned into a 'crow bar' that could, with the aid of threatened tariff retaliation, pry open foreign markets determined by the US to be closed to its exports and could be used also to remove foreign 'unfair trade practices' not defined as such by any treaty whatsoever but determined by the US to be 'unreasonable' and having adverse impact on US trade. This, in fact, is a declaration of unilateralism in defining the US trade rights and in determination to punish those who do not observe it thus violating the key principle of the GATT.

This Act also embodies a new understanding of reciprocity which is difficult from the conventional GATT approach of 'first difference' reciprocity: 'Material' reciprocity or 'Reciprocity of End Results', which results in bilateral/sectoral trade negotiations, where governments may even specify the quantities to be traded and the prices at which they may be exchanged. This, it is argued, ensures reciprocity of end results. This change in the approach of the US has been attributed to a so called 'Diminished Giant Syndrome' that the US is suffering from for the US is uninclined to be losing its dominance in the world economy. This has led to tremendous clamour in various sectors in the US which have been affected by the international competition especially by Pacific countries. The resulting belief in the US has been that the Far Eastern countries are 'not playing by the rules' and that 'level playing fields' must be established to compete with them. Therefore, the US has sought measures to create unilaterally such rules. The reciprocity principle as pursued by the US is to demand that others such as India and Japan liberalise unilaterally (or else the crow-bar will be used). The defence of this reciprocity was that in the case of Japan which has an enormous trade surplus with the US it must reduce its trade barriers faster than others. Secondly, the US has an enormous deficit with the rest of the world and therefore it is appropriate to ask others, who do not have a similar affliction to liberalise their trade unilaterally.[18] But the scope of Super 301 and Special 301 and consequently of the US unilateralism can be fully understood by the fact that a country like India, as *The Economist* puts it, having sixty times less per capita income at $ 300, contributes less than 1 per cent of trade deficit of the US and being the 27th trading partner of the US is subjected to the crow-bar treatment under the Super 301 provision of the US Omnibus Trade and Competitiveness Act 1988.[19]

This action does not stem either from the trade deficit argument for India is also suffering generally huge trade deficits and the US is its largest trading partner accounting for 15-18 per cent of India's exports and imports. This action is related to other trade policy objectives of the US. For the Second Round of 1988 Trade Act's Super 301 procedure, President Bush on April 27, 1990 pointed his finger at India for protecting its insurance industry and keeping out foreign investment. *The Economist* has effectively identified the objectives of the US in singling out India. "India has been singled out for three reasons that have nothing to do with Indian behaviour or Indian poverty, the Congress, Japan and the General Agreement on Tariffs and Trade.

That awkwardly left India, which had haughtily refused to talk at all. It is also one of several countries that is being particularly obstructive in the GATT talks. So it stays on the list, though Mr. Bush will presumably defer any actual retaliation at least until the end of the Uruguay Round". In the year 1991, India, alongwith China and Thailand, has been placed in the Special 301 list for a persistent and acute nature of the problem as seen by the US. The US can impose 100 per cent duty on imports from India. The US believes that India's Patent Act of 1970 has led to piracy, counter trade, etc. The loss according to unofficial estimates, is between $123 million and $244 million.[20]

The emerging concept of reciprocity does not confine to one sector. Its understanding could be cross-sectoral. Thus the entire economic policy of developing countries would be coming under this concept as will be seen in the cross-sectoral retaliation aspect of the Uruguay Round Negotiations.

Thus, one of the fundamental principles in international trade relations between developed and developing countries is under considerable threat although, in the declaration launching the Uruguay Round of Negotiations it was agreed by the trade negotiators from developed countries not to expect reciprocity as has already been noted.

Special and Differential Treatment

The major thrust of discussion of participation of developing countries in the trading system during the last three decades has been the necessity of providing differentiated rights and obligations to ensure that the world trading system responds to the particular needs of the developing countries.

Since 1970, the arrangements designed to promote these facilities have been referred to as instruments of a 'differential' treatment. It is not only that developing countries are not expected to observe reciprocity principle but also to receive positive discrimination in their favour to enable them to get necessary facilities.

The single most important achievement by the Framework Group of the Tokyo Round was the establishment of the idea of differential treatment for developing countries as an integral part of the GATT system.

Specific objectives were agreed to as regard the developing countries. The broad aim was to secure, in the manner and through the means set out in the Tokyo Declaration, additional benefits for the international trade of these countries, so as to achieve a substantial increase in their foreign exchange earnings, the diversification of their exports, and the acceleration of the rate of growth of trade. "Special and more favourable treatment" as provided for in the declaration, would be a prominent theme running through any area of the negotiations".[21]

Beginning with Article XVIII of GATT which provides the contracting parties from developing countries some special facility to protect the developing countries' infant industry against foreign competition by applying tariff and non-tariff restrictions, especially Article XVIII-B (as has already been argued) that permits use of quantitative restrictions for balance of payments reason, the special needs of the developing countries have been recognised.

In the declaration of contracting parties on November 28, 1979 with regard to "differential and more favourable treatment and fuller participation of developing countries", the developing countries' contracting parties have been allowed to enter into regional or global arrangements assuring for themselves mutual reduction or elimination of tariffs in accordance with the criteria or conditions which may be prescribed by the contracting parties, on products imported from one another. (See details of the Declaration in the Appendix).

Further, the declaration of the contracting parties in November 1979 has made possible grant of unilateral tariff concession by developed countries' contracting parties to those from the developing ones without seeking a waiver under Article XXV of the GATT, and as such without being bound by any time-limit as is usually prescribed in the waiver. The Generalised System of Preferences granting preferential access for products of developing countries in the markets of developed countries was accorded for ten year period waiver. The declaration of 1979 waived this time limit.

During the Tokyo Round members also embodied special and differential treatment to developing countries in some 'codes'. Differential treatment under the codes takes several forms. In many instances its substance is limited to a statement of recognition that developing countries have special needs and may face special difficulties which should be taken into account both in their application of code provisions and also in the manner in which developed countries apply the provision. Some codes, such as government procurement and standard and customs valuations, have provisions on technical assistance for developing countries. The government procurement code allows developing countries upon accession to make reservations on the application of the rules on national treatment with respect to certain products or entities on the basis of their development needs. Under subsidies code the only element of differential treatment allowed was that the developing countries could maintain export subsidies on manufactured goods as long as such subsidies did not cause serious injuries to domestic industries of importing countries.

The developed countries are also becoming increasingly interested in the markets of developing countries. They want developing countries to consolidate their liberalisation process. The developed countries have made this very clear in the Uruguay Round, essentially in two different ways. *First*, in contrast to the 1970s when developing countries were on the offensive as far as securing differential treatment was concerned they now find themselves under considerable pressure to forego these acquired rights. They are under pressure to liberalize their import regimes and offer reciprocal concessions in a number of areas. At the same time, tariff preferences, which have been considered as a gift from the developed countries under the GSP, are being granted increasingly on a restrictive basis. *Second*, the developed countries also seek important concessions in the new areas of trade in services and trade related investment measures which will be discussed later.

Graduation Concept

The disagreement existed between developed and developing countries on the question of treating all developing countries equal and extending the preferential treatment to them equally. They wanted to differentiate between the developing countries on the basis of their development. The developed countries considered this as to be concomitant with special and differential treatment. The developed countries suceeded in introducing in the enabling clause certain limitations on the availability of differential treatment. The concerned paragraph 7 states: "Less developed contracting parties expect that their capacity to make contributions or negotiated concessions or take other mutually agreed action under the General Agreement would improve with the progressing development of their economies and improvement in their trade situation and they would accordingly expect to participate more fully in the framework of rights and obligations under the General Agreement."[22] This has become known as the "graduation" principle.

There have been numerous cases where this principle has been invoked and the developing countries have insisted that this is a matter to be decided by the country concerned, on the basis of its own assessment of the situation. But, in practice, such autonomy has not always been possible. For instance, the countries have been removed from the list of beneficiaries on the ground that they have become competitive. The US action on South Korea, Hong Kong, Singapore and Taiwan is a case in point when the US excluded these countries from the list of beneficiaries.

The struggle between developed and developing countries has been whether the application of 'graduation' should be decided unilaterally by the developed countries or it should be a "mutually agreed action" as stated in para 7 of the enabling clause. The biggest problem is regarding the decision of a criterion which will transfer a developing country to a status of industrialised country. The developing countries now have to face this problem squarely because it is certain that developed countries would insist on not extending the special and differential treatment to developing countries whom they treat as having been graduated.

Draft Final Act of Uruguay Round on Special and Differential Treatment

One important aspect of the draft Final Act of Uruguay round is expected to be taken up as it is after finalisation although it is bracketed "without prejudice to the measures on special and more favourable treatment in favour of developing participants . . . (and) the participants agree that least developed participants shall be granted a grace period of years as date of entry into force of this final Act during which they will be required to apply the new commitments negotiated in the course of Uruguay Round".[23]

The developing countries are singularly trying to maintain the S and D position after Uruguay Round of Negotiations. In the closing statement, Dr. Hector Gros Espiell, Chairman of the Ministerial Meeting of the Trade Negotiations Committee, Brussels, on the pressure of developing countries declared on December 7, 1990 that more time was needed to take cognizance of the discussion of the members to arrive at a final decision on the Uruguay Round. He said: "In doing so, we are mindful of the need to conduct an effective evaluation of the extent to which the objectives relating to differential and more favourable treatment for developing countries are being attained".[24]

It is difficult to expect that after the Uruguay Round of Negotiations the special and differential treatment accorded to developing countries would remain as it is. The intellectual arguments against this facility have become loud and bold while the approaches to international negotiations have been to minimise their importance. *First*, it is argued that S and D have little economic logic underlying it and it brings no major improvement for the recipient developing countries. *Second*, the more developed countries among developing countries enjoying preferential access are the 'free riders' on the willingness of the developed countries to bear the onerous burden of liberal trade policies. *Third*, the S and D provisions help to keep the developing countries outside the mainstream of negotiations. *Fourth*, it is in the interest of the developing countries not to ask for any S and D facility but join in active negotiations and develop comparative advantage and thus be more competitive in international operations.[25] *Fifth*, this has led to the indiscipline and rising protectionism creeping in the trade policies of developed countries while at the same time the developing countries were campaigning for more differential treatment. As Martin Wolf puts it: "For the developed countries, acquiescence in demands for special treatment (by developing countries) was less politically costly than the alternative of significant non-discriminatory liberalisation on products of interest to developing countries".[26] At best, the developing countries will fight an holding operation with a serious possibility of the graduation principle becoming an effective instrument with the developed countries.

There are a number of approaches suggested to strengthen this holding operation. As some argue there must be a system to keep the development dimension adequately incorporated in the rules of international trading system. They also argue that if the development dimension were expressed in terms of appropriate unified rules rather than in terms of differential treatment with no respect for existing and future provisions, "there would still be elements of the latter".[27] Some would argue that the desire to be free of GATT discipline may be described as the "demand to be able to hurt oneself", hence, it is considered not relevant.

An alternative perspective as presented by the South Commission has been: "It is necessary . . . not to lose sight of the incontestable historical evidence that regulation of trade has been a feature of successful development in the initial stages of growth in a large number of countries including those now characterised as developed countries".

The Commission states that the commitment to the principle of differential and more favourable treatment of developing countries reaffirmed in the Ministerial Declaration of Punta Del Este should be fully honoured together with the effective operational arrangements for its implementation. "While recognising that as the economic development of these countries progresses and their trade situation improves, they should participate to an increasing degree in the rights and obligations of the trading system, this should not be unilaterally imposed by the industrial countries".[28]

It is also argued that the excessive preoccupation of the developing countries to get an S and D treatment has made them lose significantly due to the fact that they were unable to extract concessions in products of their interest.

It is significant to see that as the negotiations proceeded in the Uruguay Round the developing countries' commentators observed: "What developing countries were in practice likely to be seeking were: greater compliance with the existing rules, generally applicable improvements to certain rules, and the eradication of structural imbalances on market access negotiation. In the new areas, it appeared that accommodating the development dimension was also largely a matter of designing appropriate rules and not working out exceptions for developing countries which would almost certainly be time-bound".

Collective Approach among Developing Countries in Uruguay Round of Negotiations

The nature of decision making in the GATT has enabled a few important developing countries to play a leading role in putting across their position successfully. The contracting parties acting jointly are governed by majority vote on many matters. However, in much of GATT business there is a decided preference for a 'consensus' approach. Some experts have argued thus: "There is in fact some fear of voting, possibly with good reason, the voting structure like that of many international organisations today, for it bears little resemblance to the real power relations of the participants. The practice in the GATT generally seeks to avoid formal voting except in the case of waivers, membership and treaty amendments". A consensus approach in a way has given every country a veto and thus reduces the potential initiative to the least common denominator.[29]

It must be recognised that there is no formal group of developing countries in the GATT and negotiations under MTN did not have a specific developing countries' group negotiation. There is no Group of 77 as it is under the UN. The Group of 77 has no formal presence here as it is in the case of the IMF. The fast deteriorating international economic environment confronting developing countries has further divided them. Thus, the concept of collective bargaining was a non-starter in the Uruguay Round, the countries are grouped as SELA countries referring to developing Latin America. African countries have a group of their own and Asia has no specific group. A few Asian countries and ASEAN countries have occasionally presented their viewpoint collectively.

The Latin American countries' perception of their interest in the Uruguay Round has been dominantly influenced by the following factors. *First*, the huge international debt of a large number of Latin American countries has made them extremely vulnerable to pressures from developed countries. *Second*, since many of them are under structural adjustment programmes of the IMF and the World Bank, they are not in a position to strike a different independent path in terms of their economic policies. *Third*, there are a number of bilateral agreements such as Caribbean Initiative and the proposed Free Trade Agreement between the US and Mexico which bind them to different arrangements. *Fourth*, a number of Latin American countries are producers and exporters of agricultural products which have made them members of the Cairns Group under the Uruguay Round. There is a tradeoff that these countries expect from Uruguay Round by linking liberalisation of trade in agriculture to other aspects of Uruguay Round. *Finally*, new political leaderships in a number of countries, such as Brazil — a champion of developing countries' interest and independence — are reportedly taking a position that is much more consistent with the stance of the developed countries, especially the US. This is reflected in the statement by Mr. Marcos Castrioto Azumbiya, special representative of the Republic, General Secretary for Foreign Policy: "Brazil, in particular under the administration of President Fernando Collor, adopted, in an autonomous way, ample diversified and far-reaching measures designed to expose its industries to foreign competition and facilitate access to its markets. This was done against the background of persisting difficulties and largely adverse changes in the international environment".[30]

Regarding the African group, a few important considerations have determined their response. *First*, many of them are members of Lome Convention with the EEC. In any conflict between the objectives of Lome Convention with the collective leadership of developing countries, the requirements of Lome Convention dominate the response of the member developing countries over the demands of collective bargaining of developing countries. *Second*, a large number of them are under structural adjustment lending programme of the World Bank and the IMF assistance with conditionality and limited options for an independent stance. *Third*, in matters of economic policies, a number of them are least developed countries which in any case would be recipients of special and differential treatment. *Fourth*, the level of technological advance of these countries is limited and the service sector is not very significant. Commercial aspect of trade related intellectual property rights and liberalisation of trade in services are not therefore of any great significance. *Finally*, the large international debt of the developing countries of Africa have made them vulnerable to pressures from developed countries and international economic institutions.

Asian developing countries are clearly divided broadly into three groups, (i) ASEAN group of countries (Malaysia, Philippines, Singapore, Indonesia and Thailand); (ii) newly industrialising countries such as South Korea, Taiwan, Singapore and Hong Kong; (iii) South Asian countries in which one can have developing India and Pakistan and least developing countries Nepal, Bhutan and Bangladesh.

These countries have not successfully forged any one group for obvious differences. The ASEAN group of countries has a close collaboration with the EEC and the developed countries — USA and Japan. Further, in order to attract foreign direct investment, they have already made a number of policy changes in areas which are being negotiated in the Uruguay Round such as in services and intellectual property rights. Some of them have also changed their policies under the pressure of the US. The newly industrialising countries have already been subject to "policy reform" under the US pressure as well as due to their own national policies which are consistent with the requirements as expected to be agreed upon in the Uruguay Round. One may add here that Philippines expresses concern about the issues focussed on intellectual property rights in the Uruguay Round.

This leaves India and Pakistan. There has been some attempt on the part of these countries to cooperate in the Uruguay Round. But not much effort has been made to collaborate and there is no visible success of this effort.

Coming to the Indian case, the question is whether it will be in a position to develop the necessary capability to individually withstand the pressures and coordinate with other developing countries to formulate a common strategy. India has been a staunch opponent of a number of proposals which have been included under Uruguay Round such as services, trade related intellectual property rights and trade related investment measures. India's position has been that it opposes restrictive trade practices associated with intellectual property rights due to the adverse effects they have on transfer of technology and it is opposed to the creation of an international Investment Regime.[31] But as the Uruguay Round of Negotiations proceeded India was forced to accept negotiations on services.

Domestically, the strength of India to oppose any specific measure has greatly diminished because of serious economic problems, especially the deterioration in the balance of payments, huge budget deficits and growth of international debt and the need to borrow internationally especially from the IMF and the World Bank. Current political uncertainty which had never been there in the case of India has also had its effect in weakening India's negotiating position. It was believed in some quarters that India posed a 'counter hegemony' in the 60s and 70s. However, this strength has steadily declined thus eliminating the challenge of the former 'counter-hegemony'.

Thus, the Uruguay Round of Trade Negotiations has witnessed a steady erosion in the strength of developing countries to cooperate among themselves to extract concessions from developed countries. They are now carving out an individual approach to issues of negotiations seeking specific national benefits. In fact some have argued that the developing countries instead of getting united, are individually and in groups aligning with developed countries. This has heralded an *era of collaboration of developing countries* with the developed countries according to their individual/group interests rather than a mythical unity of all developing countries in pursuit of restructuring of the international economic order as they perceive it.

NOTES

1. Sumitra Chishti, *Foreign Trade and Economic Development of India*, (Tilburg University, Tilburg, 1985).
2. Discussion in the Seminar on UNCTAD-VII, organised by the Indian Institute of Foreign Trade, New Delhi, May 1987.
3. *UNCTAD Bulletin*, August-September 1987, p. 13.
4. Satish Jha, 'Stabilising International Commodity Prices; Too Little, Too Late', *Economic and Political Weekly*, August 19, 1989, pp. 1885-86.
5. Jackson, *Restructuring*, pp. 37-50.
6. *Draft Final Act of Uruguay Round Negotiations*, Ann Mair, (Office of Multilateral Affairs International Trade Administration), 'Balance of Payments Reform', *Uruguay Round, GATT, Update*, p. 20. *Negotiating Group on GATT Articles, Articles XII, XIV and VIII. Background Paper by the GATT Secretariat* (MTN, GNG, NGW/14).
7. Gerard Curzon, *Multilateral Commercial Diplomacy The General Agreement on Naational Commercial Policies and Techniques*, (London, Michael Joseph, 1965). For details, Richard Pomfret, *Unequal Trade, The Economics of Discriminatory Trade Policies* (Basil Blackwell, Oxford, 1988).
8. GATT Articles.
9. Robert E. Hudec, *Developing Countries in the GATT Legal System* (Trade Policy Research Centre, London, 1987), p. 82. Gerard and Victoria Curzon,' Non-discrimination and the Rise of Material Reciprocity', *Journal of World Economy*, January 1990.
10. GATT, *The Tokyo Round of Multilateral Trade Negotiations* (Geneva, 1977), p. 6. Ria Kemper, *The Tokyo Round : Results and Implications for Developing Countries* (World Bank Staff Working Paper No. 372), pp. 24-29.
11. John H. Jackson, *Restructuring the GATT System* (The Royal Institute of International Affairs, Pinter Publishers, London, 1990), pp. 25-30. Eduardo Perez Motta and Patrick Low, 'The Development Dimension in International Trade : Questions and Issues for the Participation of Developing Countries in the Multilateral Trading System' (Mimeographed).

12. Ministerial Declaration on the Uruguay Round, Part I, GATT, *Focus*, p. 4.
13. Gerard and Victoria Curzon, 'Non-discrimination and Maltilateral Reciprocity', p. 483.
14. Robert E. Hudec, *Developing Countries in the GATT Legal System*, p. 4.
15. GATT, *The Tokyo Round of Multilateral Trade Negotiations II, Supplementary Report* (Geneva, January 1990), pp. 36-37.
16. Indian Institute of Foreign Trade, *Trade Expansion Through Generalised System of Preferences* (Mimeographed), Vol I, Vol. II and Vol. III.
    UNCTAD, *Review of the Implementation, Maintenance, Improvement and Utilisation of the GSP*, TDB/C.5/32/12.
17. Gerard and Victoria Curzon, 1Non-Discrimination and the Rise of Material Reciprocity", *Journal of World Economy*, January 1990, p. 481.
18. J.N. Bhagwati, 'United States Trade Policy at the Cross-Roads', *Journal of World Economy*, January 1990 and Jagdish N. Bhagwati and Douglas A. Irwin, 'The Return of the Reciprocitarian: US Trade Policy Today', *World Economy*, June 1987.
19. "Wicked Indians", *The Economist*, 5-11, May, 1990, p. 58.
20. India Again Placed on Special 301 Hit List' *The Economic Times* April 28, 1991. Praful Bidawai, 'Special 301 Threat to Sovereignty? *Times of India* April 30, 1991.
21. GATT, *Tokyo Round of Multilateral Trade Negotiations*, (Geneva, 1979), p. 7.
22. Indian Institute of Foreign Trade, *GATT and the Uruguay Round; Special and Differential Treatment for Developing Countries* (Mimeographed, pp. 10-15) and Differential and More Favourable Treatment, Reciprocity and Fuller Participation of Developing Countries (L 14903).
23. Draft Final Act.
24. Closing Statement of Dr. Hector Gros Espiell, Chairman of the Ministerial Meeting of the Trade Negotiations Committee, Brussels, 7 December 1990 (mimeographed).
25. Martin Wolf, 'Differential and More Favourable Treatment of Developing Countries and International Trading System', *World Bank Economic Review*, Vol. I,

no. 4, September 1987, pp. 665-66.

26. Martin Wolf, 'Differential and More Favourable Treatment of Developing Countries and the International Trading System', *The World Bank Review*, Vol. no. 4 (1987), pp. 647-68.
27. Eduardo Pevez Motta and Patric Low, 'The Developmental Dimensional (Mimeographed), p. 39.
28. South Commission, *Statement*, p. 8.
29. John Jackson, *Restructuring of the GATT System*, pp. 22-25.
30. Speech by Brazil's Representative in *Uruguay Round* on 4 December, 1990.
31. See India's stand on Trade Related Investment Measures, India's Stand on Trade Related Intellectual Property Rights and India's apprehension on negotiations on Liberalization of Trade in Services. See the proceedings of the colloquium held under the auspices of Indian Institute of Foreign Trade, Vol. I and II (Mimeographed).

3

Impact of Uruguay Round on the Status of Developing Countries in the World Trading System

The Uruguay Round of Trade Negotiations is still in progress. These negotiations could have concluded on December 8, 1990 as scheduled. But the major difference between the United States and the European Economic Community on liberalization of the agricultural trade stalled the final agreement. There is every possibility of a compromise here. In most other areas, there is substantial agreement among major trading nations. Therefore, what follows in the subsequent pages is a study of the impact of the negotiations on developing countries based on the direction of the proceedings thus far rather than on the final agreement.

MARKET ACCESS

Standstill and Rollback

The eighties had experienced tremendous growth of barriers to the exports of developing countries. Many of them had been grey area measures. But a number of them could be treated as being under the scope of the GATT. At Punta-del-Este, the developing countries had sought liberalization of market access through an agreement on standstill and rollback. Under the standstill agreement it was agreed by the developed countries : (i) not to undertake any trade restrictive or distorting measures inconsistent with the provisions of the GATT or the instruments negotiated within the framework of the GATT or under its auspices; (iii) not to take any trade restrictive or distorting measures in the legitimate exercise of the GATT rights that would go beyond that which is necessary to remedy a specific situation, as provided for in the general agreement and the instruments referred to and (i) above; (iii) not to take any trade measures in such a manner as to improve a country's negotiating position.

Regarding the rollback steps, it was agreed that all trade restrictive or distorting measures inconsistent with the provisions of the General Agreement or instruments negotiated within the framework of the GATT or under its auspices shall be phased out under its auspices, or brought into conformity within an agreed time frame not later than the date of the final completion of the negotiations; and there shall be no GATT concessions requested for the elimination of these measures.[1] Developing countries had given considerable importance to achieving these objectives since they needed to expand exports of goods in which they had current comparative advantage.

Many developing countries find that Uruguay Round of negotiations have paid inadequate attention to the major issue of eliminating restriction to market access. It is considered that in the absence of adequate market access, a serious imbalance will persist between the rights and obligations of contracting parties. There are also inadequate steps taken to effect rollback commitments.

Some of the developed countries have argued that there is an apparent difficulty of determining which measures are contrary to the GATT or to instruments negotiated within the framework of the GATT or under its auspices. This stand has prevented rollback from being fully achieved.

Tariffs

A number of developing countries feel that the tariff offer at the Uruguay Round contrasts with the wide coverage and scope of the commitments embodied in their own tariff offers and their independent autonomous liberalization of trade. Further, they are also of the view that the implementation of the tariff reductions would, in certain cases, have the effect of eroding the preferential margins that benefit the product of interest to some developing countries. In order to compensate for this erosion, they think that a comprehensive reduction in tariffs of products of interest to developing countries must be made. However, no such offers have been made. Moreover, tariff concessions on products of interest to developing countries have been made contingent on *satisfactory reciprocity*.

With regard to non-tariff measures phasing out or elimination of quantitative restrictions and other measures with similar effects in pursuance of the roll back commitment remains largely unfulfilled.

Tropical Products

The Punta del Este negotiation mandate included negotiations on tropical products. The following trend had been noticed in this context.

"Negotiations shall aim at the fullest liberalization of trade in tropical products, including in their processed and semi-processed forms and shall cover both tariff and all non-tariff measures affecting trade in these products.

"Contracting parties recognize the importance of trade in tropical products to a large number of less-developed contracting parties and agree that negotiations in this area shall receive special attention, including the timing of the negotiations and the implementation as provided for in B(ii) (i.e. treated as part of single undertaking)".

Notwithstanding the importance of the products for a large number of developing countries, "progress in this area has not been good". It was expected that these negotiations will not be finalized in December 1990, but would continue at Brussels.

These negotiations have been conditioned by a number of issues raised by some of the developed countries. The progress in the negotiations in this area has been linked by them to developments in other negotiating groups and contributions by other countries, including developing countries. Further, in the course of negotiations some developed countries have argued that discussion of such products exported by the developed countries as well as agriculture must also be covered. This would introduce a *demand for reciprocity* and is, therefore, inconsistent with commitments made in the Punta del Este Declaration.[2] This would also be contrary to the entire history of negotiations since the publication of Haberler Report some 30 years ago.

Apart from this, the offers made by the developed countries leave much to be desired. For instance, in the case of African countries, the concessions are expected to result in trade expansion to the tune of $ 746 million or 3 per cent of the 1986 import value of such products in those markets. Only one third of the additional imports created (i.e. $ 245 million) would come from developing countries representing only 1.7 per cent rise in exports to these markets. The remainder of additional trade is expected to accrue to developed countries. In fact, it is estimated that the African region would experience a loss of $ 118 million, i.e. 3 per cent of their exports of 1986. African losses result of course from the erosion of preferences margins in the EEC markets and in special preferences for at least developed countries in other markets. Further, the offers are limited.[3]

Natural Resource-Based Products

The negotiations "to achieve the fullest liberalization of trade in natural resource-based products, including in their semi-processed and processed form have not proceeded to the extent expected. The prospects for this negotiating group to meet its mandate do not appear encouraging. In fact, the Chairman of the Group has proposed an institutional arrangement for negotiations on non-tariff measures and subsidies in this area till the end of 1991 along with a formula to reduce/eliminate tariff barriers despite the expectations expressed at the Montreal Meeting. "Given the interrelationship of issues raised in natural resource-based products and other areas of negotiations in the Uruguay Round, it is necessary to ensure that the progress in negotiations on natural resource-based products is consistent with other related areas".[4]

The reason for the tardy progress in this important sector that is of interest to developing countries is that the proposals made by the major developed countries to include measures relating to both access to and management of the supply of natural resources, as well as to extend the group's coverage to product areas not envisaged in the preparatory process of the launching of the Uruguay Round.

Textiles

The textile sector has been one of the most important sectors from the point of view of developing countries. Since this sector has been outside the GATT, there has been an endeavour to integrate it within the GATT and the scheme of liberalization of trade leading to substantial improvement in their export earnings. They expected to decrease appreciably the scope for restrictions, accelerate the phase-out of the restrictive trade regime of Multi Fibre Agreement (MFA) and decrease protection to domestic industries of MFA users as well as progressively and selectively eliminate, safeguard and limit resort to trade harassment measures. But, there has not been much progress in this direction.

Safeguard Measures

With regard to safeguard measures, there are a few positive elements in the understandings. The draft agreement contains that obligation as causality to ensure that injury to domestic industry should be attributed to increased imports. It also includes improved provisions relating to determination of injury, preference for tariffs and quantitative restrictions, and commitment to eliminate 'grey area' measures such as voluntary export restrictions or to bring them into conformity with the proposed safeguard agreements. But these are totally nullified by other provisions. On the question of 'selectivity', there has been disagreement. There has been a serious attempt at legitimization of discriminatory safeguard actions against imports from 'selected' countries. "The EC is strongly advocating selectivity in the application of safeguards, that is temporary import barriers imposed in order to protect domestic industries at risk. If this proposal is accepted the consequential restrictions would be made essentially against countries from the third world rather than against those from developed countries. It has been an accepted international principle so far that safeguards should be applied to imports from all sources and not selectively.[5] If selectivity is legitimised, the above stated objective would not only be met, but would have adverse consequences for the GATT as a whole and for developing countries in particular.[6]

Thus, the market access to exports of developing countries is still open to a bilateral and selective approach and expectation of reciprocity. In fact, the slow and inadequate progress made in the case of textiles, tropical products and natural resource-based products also proves the priorities that dominate multilateral trade negotiations. The interests of developing countries have been unimportant all these years in multilateral trade negotiations. They appear to remain the same in the Uruguay Round as well.

Liberalization of International Trade in Agriculture and Developing Countries

All the multilateral trade negotiations before Uruguay Round did not consider agriculture comprehensively for negotiations — agriculture as distinct from tropical products and natural resource-based products, include cereals, meat, dairy products, oilseeds/vegetable oils (non-biological) and sugar in Uruguay Round negotiations of agriculture. These products account for the bulk of world trade in agricultural products in value terms. For decades, contracting parties of the GATT have turned a blind eye to the various trade distorting agricultural policies of contracting parties. This has been particularly true of a number of developed countries who have systematically protected their agriculture from the international competition. The OECD estimated that the trade distorting policies had cost consumers and taxpayers in industrialized countries $ 245 billion in 1989. As a result of protection of agriculture, a number of developing countries lost their market, for instance, in wheat, meat and sugar. The protectionist policy of developed countries resulted in the developing countries exporting sugar losing their share in world trade. In 1967 the developed countries were net importers of sugar. Due to the domestic policies, their domestic production of sugar doubled.[7] By the mid-eighties the EEC emerged as the second largest exporter of sugar. In a number of products, a large number of developing countries are net importers for instance of cereals.

The Punta del Este Ministerial Declaration defined the goals of the agricultural negotiations as "to achieve greater liberalization of trade in agriculture, and bring all measures affecting import access and export competition under strengthened and more operationally effective GATT rules and disciplines..."

The mid-term review agreement of April 1989 set the parameters for the subsequent negotiating process that was slated to be completed by the end of 1990. It was stated in this agreement that there was "a broad measure of consensus that agricultural policies should be more responsive to international market signals in order to meet the objective of liberalization of international trade and that support and protection should be progressively reduced and provided in a less distorting manner".

The agreement document stated: "The long-term objective of the agricultural negotiations is to establish a fair and market-oriented agricultural trading system and that a reform process should be initiated through the negotiations of commitments on support and protection and through the establishment of strengthened and more operationally effective GATT rules and disciplines.".

This marked a significant movement from the original negotiating mandate of achieving trade liberalization, toward disciplining the form and degree of government intervention.[8] The participating Ministers stated, under the Mid-Term Review Agreement, that "the particular needs and conditions of developing countries should be fully taken into account at all stages of negotiations". They agreed that special and differential treatment to developing countries was "an integral part of the negotiation" particularly as regard new rules and disciplines. They also recognized that government assistance, whether direct or indirect, to encourage agricultural and rural development was "an integral part of the development programme of developing countries". The Ministers also agreed that "ways should be developed to take into account the possible negative effects of the reform process on net food-importing developing countries".

The major issues that have been under negotiation include the fundamental question being negotiated in relation to domestic agricultural support by the government and the forms of government support. The US and Cairns Group (Argentina, Australia, Brazil, Canada, Chile, Colombia, Fiji, Hungary, Indonesia, Malaysia, New Zealand, the Philippines, Thailand and Uruguay) want the phase-out of some specific policies and measures. This has been spelt out clearly by the US in the category of 'red light' as those to be phased out, 'yellow light' as those to be disciplined and 'green light' as those to be permitted. The red category includes administered price policies designed to result in domestic prices higher than the prevailing world market prices, income support policies linked to production and marketing, subsidies in inputs or investment not provided to producers or processors on an equal basis and transportation subsidies other than permitted.

The European Community proposed that agricultural support levels be bound under the GATT, with reference to a Support Measurement Unit (SMU). The SMU is based on the Product Subsidy Equivalent (PSE), as developed by the OECD. The PSE is an index of the income benefit that producers derive from policies. It includes government budget outlays and other financial benefits to farmers, such as those derived from restrictive border measures. These are calculated as the difference between domestic farm-gate prices and representative world market prices. The SMU is the PSE, adjusted by:

(a) excluding payments which represent a direct and immediate compensation for the reduction of the use of production factors;
(b) taking into account production control measures; and

(c) using a fixed external reference price, with which to compare domestic farm-gate prices.

The purpose of fixing an external price, instead of using a variable representative world market price, is to focus the SMU reduction in terms of domestic support levels.

The EC specifies that the SMU would cover:

(a) measures to support market prices;
(b) direct payments linked to production or to factors of production;
(c) measures aimed at reducing input costs which are commodity specific, or which can be feasibly calculated by commodity; and
(d) all measures affecting support levels, whether applied internally, or at the border.

The commitments to reduce support would be expressed as a percentage reduction of SMU, calculated both on a unit and total basis. They could vary by product group. Commitment would be adjusted according to developments in world market prices. This could mean a possible halt to support reduction in the event of high prices on the world market. The EC also foresees a provision to ensure that adjustments are comparable among different countries, despite differences in inflation rate.

Reductions would be measured against the reference year of 1986. They would take place over five years in a first state. The absolute amount of reduction of the SMU would in principle be the same each year of the agreed period, before being adjusted upwards or downwards in order to take into account trends in world markets. The market situation would be studied during the fourth year, to determine the subsequent extent and rate of reduction in support.

Under the EC proposal, individual country schedules in terms of SMU reductions would be bound. Contracting parties would not necessarily need to identify national policy instruments they intended to adjust to comply with the binding of their support levels — they would be binding an overall number or percentage. But the EC does allow that they could be requested to do so. The Community itself has stated its readiness to indicate, if necessary, what kind of changes in policy instruments, including border protection, it would apply to reduce the SMU as agreed.

The reduction of support in terms of the SMU would apply only to the main agricultural commodity sectors. For the EC, these include: cereals, rice, sugar, oilseeds and oleaginous fruit, dairy products, beef and veal, pigmeat, eggs and poultrymeat. Processed products incorporating these would be covered by reduction commitments, through the use of transformation or incorporation coefficients. "Equivalent commitments" should be undertaken for other products.

Other Proposals

Other proposals seek to exempt from reduction commitments certain policies undertaken for specific objectives. Austria, Japan, South Korea, the Nordic countries and Switzerland believe that the reduction commitments should not cover domestic subsidies accorded in the pursuit of non-trade objectives such as the protection of the environment, land use, rural employment and food security. Switzerland proposes that domestic subsidies granted by countries agreeing to guarantee minimum market access should be permitted provided that the products thus subsidized are not exported and the market access undertakings are duly fulfilled. Japan, moreover, would exclude from AMs reduction those products with a high import ratio to consumption.

Developing countries believe that the domestic subsidies they apply, which are necessary for development purposes, should be excluded from reduction commitments. Colombia and Thailand have proposed that developing countries should not be barred from maintaining support policies, which are designed to replace illicit narcotic crops with other cash crops.

It is important to state the vital role of agriculture in developing countries. As the South Commission has argued: "In framing new rules for trade in agriculture, we must not lose sight of the real developmental role of agriculture in the Third World countries, which makes it fundamentally different from that of developed countries. In a large number of developing countries, agriculture provides a livelihood for the majority of the population, who would find it extremely difficult to shift to other activities. Small and uneconomic holdings predominate. Owing to the acute pressure of population and lack of alternative job opportunities, agriculture is characterised by both overcrowding and low productivity. Chronic poverty afflicts a large number of small and marginal farmers and a growing number of landless agricultural workers.

"Measures designed to increase the productivity of small and marginal farmers and to provide new on-farm and off-farm employment opportunities in rural areas to absorb the landless workers constitute an essential component of a viable agricultural development strategy in a predominantly agrarian economy. It is clear that the solution of these problems will demand a strong leadership role from the State and cannot be left to the care of market forces. In particular, market processes cannot deal with the chronic problems of rural poverty as the rural poor are often not part of the market system.

"Moreover, in a situation characterized by vast imperfections of factor and product market in the rural areas, the State has to intervene actively to promote the cause of equitable development. For example, small and marginal farmers are greatly handicapped on account of their inability to secure access to credit for purchases of inputs. Even when credit is available the riskiness associated with lending to small and marginal farmers induces money lenders to charge often usurious rates of interest. Such high rates of interest constitute a serious disincentive for investment in farm improvements. Thus, for equitable and balanced development to be achieved, it is necessary for the Government to intervene to reduce the cost of credit for rural borrowers. Such support should not be construed as a distortion or a subsidy."

Historically, farm price support and procurement measures have played a very important role in stimulating agricultural production in developed countries. By now there is undoubtedly a strong case for scaling down for such protectionism in the developed countries; conversely, however, the role of agricultural support measures for the economic development of developing countries must be fully recognized.[9]

The implications of these proposals to developing countries depend on the extent of the special and differential treatment granted. The real question is whether and to what extent developing countries can maintain or will have to reduce, if not eliminate, their support policies which are directly tied to production or prices such as specially administered price policies, income support linked to production and subsidies on inputs or investment which are commodity specific.

With regard to market access the Cairns Group and the US have identical proposals. For instance, with regard to tariffication India along with Japan has not agreed for tariffication while the US and Cairns Groups want tariffication for all products. Thus the expectations of developing countries have been different on agriculture in the Uruguay Round.

Further, it is important to note that negotiation on agriculture has brought into focus that alignment of developed and developing countries. For instance, the Group consisting of a few large developing countries such as Brazil and Argentina and also smaller developing countries joined together with the US to press for their demands. The internal support offer of the Cairns Group and the US are similar: reduction in subsidies to at most 75 per cent over 10 years from 1991-92 with base year 1988 (Cairns Group), US offers no less than 75 per cent over 10 years from 1991-92 on a 1986 to 1988 average base period for commodity specific support, a 30 per cent reduction over the same period.

Implications of Proposals for Developing Countries

The lack of effective multilateral discipline over agricultural import restrictions and export subsidies has largely favoured the industrialized countries. Their support policies have had a distorting impact on world trade. Effective rules and disciplines over these practices would offer improved market opportunities for developing countries. An improved contractual basis for their trade with developed countries is also required. But, the role of the State intervention in agriculture is vital to developing countries. The results of these negotiations should not prevent state action in developing countries in agriculture to achieve developmental goals. In this context, the importance of special and differential treatment acquires substantial significance.

Modalities for Special and Differential Treatment for Developing Countries

The following recapitulates the modalities for special and differential treatment for developing countries on the basis of the proposals and considerations.

(1) Flowing from the general principles governing the negotiations developing countries will participate in the agricultural reform process in accordance with their individual trade, financial and development needs and capabilities.

(2) The following measures will inter alia be excluded from reduction commitments, whether expressed in terms of specific policies or an aggregate measurement of support; income support policies linked to development objectives; environmental and conservation programmes; disaster assistance; domestic food aid; marketing programmes, market information, market promotion, inspection and grading, general research, extension and education services; resource retirement to facilitate transition; and stockpiling of food reserves.

(3) Developing countries will not be subject to reduction commitments with respect to governmental measures forming an integral part of their individual development

programmes, including inter alia aid for infrastructure development.

(4) Developing countries will not be subject to reduction commitments with respect to support policies designed to replace illicit narcotic crops with other cash crops.

(5) In case where individual developing countries undertake commitments to reduce trade distorting support and protection to the agricultural sector, special and differential treatment will apply. A longer period of time, possibly with a grace period, and greater flexibility, will be accorded to developing countries in implementing their reduction commitments on internal support and protection against imports.

(6) Developing countries shall retain the possibility to resort to export prohibitions and restrictions consistent with inter alia Article XI:(2) and Article XX(h) of GATT.

(7) Developing countries shall retain the possibility to resort to protective measures consistent with Article XVIII of GATT.

(8) Developing countries shall be specifically authorized under Article XI of GATT to apply quantitative restrictions to ensure stable and adequate supplies of basic wage goods indigenously.

(9) Due credit shall be given to contributions by developing countries to the agricultural reforms process, including any loss of preferential margins or shares experienced as a result of global liberalization.

(10) Developing countries shall undertake commitments with respect to export subsidies consistent with their individual competitive and development needs. They shall be

accorded longer time-frames and flexibility in implementing their commitments.

(11) Where risk allows, developing countries shall have longer periods of time to comply with international standards with respect to sanitary and phytosanitary measures. They shall receive technical assistance for improving their national sanitary and phytosanitary conditions.

(12) Developed countries shall reduce on an accelerated basis their internal support and trade barriers on products of priority export interest to developing countries.

(13) Existing tariffs in developed countries shall be reduced to zero or low levels, on the basis of a formula with a harmonizing effect. Developed countries shall not be allowed to take new non-tariff measures. Existing non-tariff measures should be converted into tariffs, subject to maximum ad valorem equivalents, and reduced to zero or low levels.

(14) Developed countries shall support their agricultural sector for purposes of carrying out non-trade objectives including food security, in a manner de-coupled from production and trade effects.

(15) The terms and conditions of access in individual developed country markets for products originating from developing countries shall be bound under the General Agreement.

(16) All food aid shall be provided on a grant basis. It shall respond to the immediate dietary and long-term development needs of the recipient countries.

(17) In the process of implementing long-term reform of agriculture, the specific needs of the

net food-importing developing countries shall be taken into account, particularly those of the least-developed countries. Appropriate compensation and other measures shall be provided for higher food costs in these countries, to enhance their capacity to increase agricultural production. Additional financial resources should be made available for these purposes, which will require appropriate action by and through other multilateral organizations. Eligibility for compensation along the above lines shall be limited to those developing countries that face critical shortage of basic foodstuff (stable food consumed by the low-income segment of the population), critical balance of payments problems, and critical shortages of foreign exchange reserves.

(18) Developed countries shall not use food as a means of political pressure.

(19) Developed countries shall grant compensation to developing countries for trade loss suffered as a result of sanitary and phytosanitary measures applied against them, which were not supported by scientific evidence.[10]

The above modalities for special and differential treatment have been formulated primarily in terms of developed countries and developing countries. Depending on the outcome of the final package, developing countries may need to pursue specific modalities, either individually or in combination, in the interest of the development of their agricultural sectors. This reflects the manner in which the options have been formulated before the Negotiating Group. Consideration might also be given to formulating modalities for taking into account the development dimension in the rules and disciplines of the General Agreement in a manner which avoids this dichotomy.

The agricultural negotiations are also among the most complex issues being negotiated. Central to the debate is what should be the proper role of government intervention in an economic sector, its form and degree. It is the goal of some participants to achieve greater harmonization, if not standardisation, of all governmental measures that can influence competition between domestic and foreign producers and products.

The catalyst for reforming the agricultural trading system under the General Agreement was the increased cost burden on the industrialized countries over the last decade to support their agricultural sectors. They have already taken measures to reduce these costs. The challenge ahead is to assure under the agricultural trade reform package that the industrialized countries do not continue to reduce their costs in a manner detrimental to developing countries. Reductions in support must be the vehicle for enhanced agricultural productivity and trading opportunities for developing countries. But it also raises a host of questions on their domestic agricultural policies linked with international understanding. The implications of this to various developing countries cannot be made. But one thing is certain that agriculture which was not on the agenda of international negotiations has now become an important item of international negotiations whose implications to a number of developing countries' policies on agriculture are unpredictable.

Liberalization of International Trade in Services

Introducing the liberalization of international trade

in services in the negotiations package of multilateral trade negotiations under the auspices of the GATT by the US in the early eighties was one of the most controversial issues of the negotiations. Very few countries were prepared to discuss this issue. However, the EEC and Japan agreed for negotiation in due course. But the developing countries were reluctant to agree to bring their services sector under international negotiations, especially under the GATT.

It is useful to see the different perceptions that forced the developed countries, led by the US, to take an aggressive approach while the developing countries, led by India, Brazil and Egypt sought to keep the issue of services outside the negotiations.

The developed countries, especially the US, considered that the services sector had become important not only in their economies but also in their inter national trade. The share of the services sector in the gross national product of developed countries was as high as 70 per cent in some cases. Their contribution to employment in developed countries had been higher. The international trade in services is not as large as popularly believed. Only 8 per cent of services is traded in the world. The world trade in services has actually grown less than talked about during 1970-85. International trade in services has increased at a rate of 22.4 per cent per annum as compared to 20.4 per cent per annum for trade in goods. The share of services in international trade declined during the decade 1970-80 from 16 per cent to 13 per cent while the contribution of trade in services to GDP and balance of payments had grown. The proportion of export of services to GDP in the US had gone up from 3.6 per cent to 4.4 per cent within a period of five years (1980-85). This had made the developed countries, especially the

US, to believe that the restrictions to trade in services have been responsible for the limited growth of international trade of its services.

The growth of services in developed countries can be attributed to the following factors. *First*, there have been technological developments which have resulted in the emergence of new services in the field of information, data processing and telecommunications. In brief, these developments have dynamised the traditional production-related services sector as well as the non-production related services. *Second*, it is argued that growth of services can be attributed to high income elasticity that the services sector enjoys. *Third*, the delinking of production services from production with tremendous technological developments has also been considered an important factor for the growth of services.

This delinking of production services has taken place because of a few developments. *First*, inhouse services have been increasingly replaced by the purchase of specialized services from other firms. *Second*, service operations provided within the firm have tended to be sold to outside clients, a process which usually leads to the establishment of externalised subdivisions that then sell the services both back to the parent firm and in the open market. This process of externalization has had the additional result of making specialised producer services more available to small and medium-sized enterprises thus in turn facilitating the establishment of more specialised service firms.

This has led many developed countries, especially the US, to believe that they have achieved a comparative advantage. Hence, they have visualised that liberalization of international trade in services must be an integral part of the entire process of liberalization of international trade including merchandise as a grand tradeoff with the international interest and the interest of the offering country. This was particularly the position of the US. It is emphasised that if the US had to yield on goods it was fair to ask others to yield on services and now the US has acquired the comparative advantage in services.[11]

Developing countries like India and Brazil initially opposed the inclusion of services for negotiations in the Uruguay Round. Their apprehensions have been based on a number of considerations. *First,* they feared that they have not acquired adequate knowledge on various services and the impact of liberalization on them. *Second,* some of the services such as banking, transport and insurance are in an infant stage of development. They need protection. *Third,* since the state plays an important role in a number of services sectors such as banking, insurance and transport to achieve specific development objectives in developing countries sudden liberalization of international trade in these sectors would result in possible distortions of the objectives of development. *Fourth,* the services sector is dominated by the transnational corporations which have, over the years, increased their hold through mergers and acquisitions. This is a predominant feature in banking, media and advertising. Even the entertainment world is subject to mergers. The trade in a number of services sectors is based not only on the quantifiable price factor; it includes quality of services, famous trade marks, the suppliers of renowned or reputed, better organized and more powerful distribution networks. Thus the international trade in services is characterised by the imperfection of the market and the limited role of competition. This has led to various restrictive business practices in the services sector. Developing countries have apprehensions that these restrictive practices adopted by the TNCs would influence them adversely. In the decades of sixties and seventies there was a serious attempt to regulate transnational corporations and private monopolies. Although there was no consensus on the ways of achieving the objective of limiting the adverse effects of anticompetitive as well as unsocial behaviour of these monopolies, one could argue that there were attempts to develop codes of conduct and rules and regulations to prevent restrictive business practices. In the Uruguay Round a number of developing countries have raised this issue. For instance, the Indian presentation on trade related intellectual property rights and trade related investment measures specifically focussed on this issue.

The importance of RBDs as a possible barrier to trade in goods and services was clearly recognised by all states which adopted the set of principles and rules of the control of restrictive business practices which was set as objective number one of the Code;

"To ensure that restrictive business practices do not impede or negate the realization of benefits that should arise from the liberalization of tariff and non-tariff barriers affecting world trade, particularly those affecting the trade and development of developing countries".[12]

In the context of trade liberalization of services also this issue has been raised for the services sector and, as has been discussed, has been dominated by the TNCs. There is also ample evidence to show that TNCs in various sectors indulge in restrictive business practices.[13]

Fifth, the developing countries would like to include in liberalization in trade in services such sectors of their interest. For instance, they have been asking to include labour in the liberalization of trade in services.

Sixth, since many developing countries suffer from adverse balance of payments in a large number of services, the liberalization of trade in services would further aggravate their balance of payments deficits.[14]

Finally, they considered that the negotiations should be organized not in the GATT, but in other institutions which are looking after various services sectors. They had feared that by bringing services under the auspices of the GATT, the developed countries would acquire two important advantages: (a) They would be able to link the negotiations with the intra-service sector and be effective, and (b) they would also extend their linkages to merchandise trade leading to various difficulties to developing countries.

Despite their reservations the developing countries were, in a way, forced to negotiate this sector if they wanted to be included in multilateral trade negotiations. Developing countries ultimately agreed to participate in the MTNs on trade in services when it was decided at the Punta del Este Ministerial Meeting in September 1986 that:

(a) Negotiations on trade in services would be conducted in an ad hoc juridical frame of reference separate from the legally distinct negotiations on trade in goods, leaving the question open as to whether an international regime of trade in services was indeed needed, and if so, whether it should be within the GATT framework, or as a separate Code of its own,

(b) Promoting the development of developing

countries would be regarded as an integral part of the objectives for negotiations, these are designed to promote economic growth of all trading partners and the developments of developing countries through expansion of trade in services under conditions of transparency and progressive liberalization,

(c) The framework would respect the policy objectives of national laws and regulations applying to services.[15]

Hence, a separate track of negotiations was initiated with the ostensible deference to developing countries' position and focussing on the importance of recognizing the needs of development. The agreement stated: "Negotiations in this area shall aim to establish a multilateral framework and rules for trade in services, including elaboration of possible disciplines for individual sectors, with a view to ensuring expansion of such trade under conditions of transparency and progressive liberalization and as means of promoting economic growth of all trading partners and the development of developing countries. Such framework shall respect policy objectives of national laws and regulations applying to services and shall take into account the work of relevant international organizations".[16]

It was also agreed that the GATT procedures and practices shall apply to these negotiations. The GATT Secretariat, it was further agreed, would support the negotiations.

A draft agreement on services has been negotiated in the Uruguay Round. The General Agreement on Trade in Services and General Agreement on financial Services have been submitted for finalization. It may be noted here that the US which was the initiator of these discussions is now having some reservations in a number of sectors of services.

The negotiations have been held at two levels: one relates to the text of the framework Agreement while the other covers the number of sectors. It is feared by some developing countries that negotiations have suffered serious setbacks mainly owing to the attempt to dilute the most favoured nation clause to its minimum expression and to make it conditional as well as because of the intention to exclude important sectors of interest to developing countries from the scope of application of the framework.

As one of the trade officials of the US government has put it, "Most of the discussion focussed on the controversy over how the GATT principle of 'Most Favoured Nation' (MFN) treatment would be applied to services". The MFN principle states that all signatories to an agreement should receive the best treatment accorded by one signatory to any other GATT member.

"Negotiations on concrete market access commitments for services had not gotten off the ground throughout the entire four years of the Uruguay Round without concrete market access commitments. MFN would bind only the United States and other countries that have open service markets, while providing closed market countries with a free ride".[17]

The US attempted to re-establish the linkage between the MFN and market access commitments by proposing that MFN should not automatically apply to all services, but rather should apply only to specific commitments that countries make, what the US commentators call "progressive MFN". All other countries opposed this. But it has forced them to make market access proposal, agreeing that MFN could be applied fully but on the condition that sufficient market access and national treatment commitments are negotiated. Thus it retained the linkages between MFN and commitments. This forced other countries to negotiate on this thus making negotiations of market access and national treatment as an integral part of at least "a formula for assuring that such commitments can be negotiated in the future".[18]

In the commentary on draft agreement, the Chairman of Group on Negotiating Services has expressed the concern of countries in Article II on most favoured nations treatment.[19] Some developing countries have also been worried by the proposals of the EEC with respect to a "freeze" on existing access and national treatment conditions in response to the US proposal for conditional MFN and sectoral agreements.

The ultimate outcome could be sectoral and bilateral negotiations which will keep the developing countries in a quandary. These developing countries who could offer reciprocal privileges, can afford to get absorbed while those who cannot may be left out. In the entire draft agreement there is no emphasis on special and differential treatment while Article IV of the draft agreement states that the strengthening of the domestic services capacity, its efficacy, competition, improvement of their access to (technology and) to distribution channels and information networks and special status to least developed countries. There is a proposal that the least developed countries would not be asked to make concessions.

The implementation of this Agreement when it is signed has to be left to an organization something that will be discussed later.

Trade-Related Intellectual Property Rights

For the first time, under the auspices of the GATT, the trade related aspects of intellectual property rights have been negotiated. The mandate of the relevant negotiating groups is : "In order to reduce the distortions and impediments to international trade, and taking into account the need to promote effective and adequate protection of intellectual property rights, and to ensure that measures and procedures to enforce intellectual property rights do not themselves become barriers to legitimate trade, the negotiations shall aim to clarify GATT provisions and elaborate as appropriate new rules and disciplines.

"Negotiations shall aim to develop a multilateral framework of principles, rules and disciplines dealing with international trade in counterfeit goods, taking into account work already undertaken in the GATT. These negotiations shall be without prejudice to other complementary initiatives that may be taken in the world Intellectual Property Rights organization and elsewhere to deal with these matters".

While the debate on counterfeit goods dates back to the Tokyo Round, the inclusion of the need for effective protection of intellectual property rights has been brought in for the first time under multilateral trade negotiations. The GATT does not address TRIPs in such a comprehensive manner, although there are a few provisions. Article IX.6 requires that contracting parties cooperate to prevent the use of trade names "in such a manner as to misrepresent the true origin of a product". Article XII (C) (iii) states that the "import restrictions should not prevent compliance with patent, trade mark, copyright or similar procedures". Article XVIII permits developing countries to take protective measures to promote economic development and contain an identical similar provision. Article XX, sub-paragraph (d), is a general agreement for actions taken to secure compliance with patent, trade mark, and copyright laws, provided that these laws themselves are not inconsistent with the agreement. While these provisions allow discussion of intellectual property rights under the GATT, the US position has been to make intellectual property protection a legitimate topic of concern in the multilateral trading system.[20]

This is the most vexed question in negotiations between the developed and the developing countries for the aim of this is to protect the rights of technology producers. There is a fundamental difference in the approaches of the developed countries and the developing countries. The developed countries want comprehensive and substantive rules to be formulated for technology protection while developing countries believe that no such mandate was given under the Uruguay Round.

The developed countries, especially the US. believe that violation of intellectual property rights has been very costly to it resulting in huge losses on the one hand and curtailment of their competitiveness on the other. The US International Trade Commission estimated that in 1986 alone the intellectual property rights violations had cost American industries $ 23.8 billion by way of loss of domestic sales and royalties. This is estimated to be 14 per cent of the merchandise trade deficit, and 1.5 per cent of the country's gross national product.[21] Another estimate is that the worldwide losses of US industries because of inadequate protection of intellectual property rights have totalled an estimated $ 60 billion.[22] The US is, therefore, seen to justify its demand for bringing intellectual property rights within the framework of the GATT to enforce stricter intellectual property rights.

Many developed countries, led by the US, want a comprehensive agreement under the GATT which encompasses protection for all areas of technology property (patents, trade marks, copyrights, etc.), effective enforcement measures (both at the border and internally) and effective dispute settlement provisions.

Apart from the counterfeiting of goods, trade related intellectual property rights negotiations have gone far to take into consideration various elements of national policies on technology transfer. This is in particular reference to products, compulsory licensing and public interest.

Protection of patents has been one of the major ways of protecting the rights of the inventor and the seller. Very often this protection offered by the patent stifles the growth of technology in developing countries. This happens because of two major factors. The patent owner rarely wants to transfer his knowledge. Further, he uses the protection offered by law to prevent any competition coming from anybody by importing goods produced by the patent. Thus the developing country can scarcely expect building up of technology base within this national frontier. Hence, many developing countries insist that the patent holder produces the product within the country within a specified period of time, say, three years, as has been the case in India. Also many counties reduce the period of protection, so as to reduce the stranglehold of monopoly in technology. Various national legislations seek to curb this by reducing the period of patent. For instance, in the case of India, the patent protection granted for food, medicines, drugs and agrochemicals is 7 years and other products are offered patent protection of 14 years. In order to reduce the adverse effect of monopoly in the patent protection on indigenous technology growth, some of them offer patent protection only for the process while product is not patented. In addition to this, various governments in developing counties try to limit the evil effects of monopoly effects of a technology supplier through restricting the scope of the patent by introducing compulsory licensing. In those cases where patent monopoly is likely to affect the cause of the public interest, the government keeps the prerogative of breaking the patent monopoly.

Under the trade related intellectual property rights, the developed countries, especially the US, would like to limit the authority of national governments to legislate on these issues through the agreement on this subject under the GATT. It is believed that the World Intellectual Property Rights Organization (WIPRO) has been ineffective in protecting the interest of the holders of patents.

Some of the developing countries, led by India and Brazil, had opposed these efforts to tighten standards of protection because they view this as a matter for countries to decide for themselves according to their development objectives. These countries would like to retain as much flexibility as possible for national laws. For them GATT's involvement should be limited to border measures to address copyright, piracy and trade mark and counterfeiting. As India argued at one time, "The protection of intellectual property rights has no direct or significant relationship to international trade. It is because substantive issues of intellectual property rights are not germane to international trade that GATT itself has played only a peripheral role in this area and the international community has established other specialized agencies to deal with them. It would, therefore, not be appropriate to establish within the framework of the GATT any new rules and disciplines pertaining to standards and principles concerning the availability , scope and use of intellectual property rights".[23]

It is also argued that while the GATT's mission has always been to prevent, or at least to circumscribe, countries' efforts to protect their domestic industries, "Now in the TRIPs area, the GATT is being called upon to extend protection, not to restrict it. Of course, the concepts of protection are different in the two cases. Proponents of the TRIPs negotiation would argue that protection of intellectual property is needed to permit the owners of that property to export the products that embody their innovations. Therefore, intellectual property protection, despite its name, is to be pro-trade. On the other hand, one could also take the view that the GATT's mission has been to promote the free international flow of goods in trade, and that if that mission is indeed extended to intellectual property, it should also promote the free international flow of ideas. From this perspective, again, the goals of the Uruguay Round Negotiations in restricting this free flow may be viewed as perverse".[24]

Despite these varying approaches, the TRIPS have been negotiated and an agreement has been drafted although there is no final acceptance by the negotiating countries. Over the period of negotiations, it can be argued, the opposition of developing countries to TRIPS has been steadily reduced. For instance, it is believed that Brazil is not a serious opponent: The other Latin American countries hold the view that while protection may be granted, public interest issues must also be protected. The ASEAN countries underline the importance of curbing the unilateral interpretation of what constitutes effective intellectual property rights protection. They are equally strongly committed to the concept of public interest. China also accepted the concept of establishing "relevant rules within the mandate of the Punta del Este Ministerial Declaration."[25] But India seems to have held on to its orginal position. "We have entered into negotiations in the area of TRIPs with a clear reservation on the question of lodgement of the outcome. Nearly two years of negotiation on norms and standards have convinced us that there is no place in GATT for an agreement concerning that aspect. They raise issues of policy spanning over diverse areas of technology, ethics, culture and economic development. GATT is concerned with trade policies and should remain as such".[26]

The developing countries with their limited resources cannot effectively argue in fifteen negotiating groups and for many developing countries choosing the areas of interest and a possible tradeoff with the developed countries is a complex and difficult task. It is believed that the Cairns Group of countries would be ready to make fundamental concessions in TRIPs area if they achieve good results in agriculture. The ASEAN countries may want a concession in foreign direct investment. They are also concerned on antidumping and safeguard measures. China wanted to become a contracting party. Hence, it was not very vocal. Thus, each developing country had its own perception and national interests to pursue.

Apart from protection, one more area of TRIPS has been a subject of great concern to developing countries. There have been a number of Conventions regarding dispute settlement in intellectual property rights. If the country did not comply with the agreement, the most that other parties could do under the Conventions was to withdraw national treatment they gave to citizens of the country which was a violator of the rules. By bringing it to the GATT, the developed countries would like to ensure that any country which does not adhere to an agreed protection regime may be subjected to 'cross retaliation' or 'cross sectoral retaliation' by credible and effective punishment for access to markets through cross linkages.

The thrust of the negotiation and the draft is towards:

(a) a comprehensive agreement on TRIPs based on upward harmonization and adoption of uniform standards coupled with commitments on strict enforcement; and
(b) lodgement of the agreement in the GATT.

The developing countries, as has already been discussed, would hold on to only trade related aspects although there is no unanimity; along with it they also seek public policy considerations by providing flexibility in the substantive obligation.

Further, it may be noted that not much attention has been given to restrictive business practices of technology suppliers. This is in contrast to efforts made at UNCTAD to bring about a code on Restrictive Business practices. No doubt Article 43 of the Draft Final Act refers to restrictive business practices and the need to eliminate them. But the entire clause is in brackets having no agreement on that issue. It may be noted that the failure to evolve an agreed code on Restrictive Business Practices was mainly because of the objections raised by the developed countries.

The final draft of Uruguay Round includes distinctly two different approaches to this issue: one, Trade Related Aspects of Intellectual Property Rights, including counterfeit goods, and, the other, on trade in counterfeit and pirated goods. Those who seek a single agreement encompassing all areas of negotiations envisage that this would be implemented as an integral part of the GATT. Others feel that the part on counterfeit would be implemented by the GATT and other intellectual property protection would be implemented by the relevant international organisation. This difference of approach could be resolved only when the institutional set-up is finally decided.

But the manner in which the negotiations have proceeded is a cause for serious concern to developing countries. This agreement would result in

(a) increase in the costs of production and importation of goods in developing countries on account of higher costs of technology,
(b) tightening of the monopolistic control over knowledge and technology,
(c) adverse effect on trade liberalization;
(d) upsetting of the balance between the protection of intellectual property rights and their use for promotion of global welfare, making developing countries vulnerable to cross sectoral retaliation; and
(e) most significantly bringing under international dicipline a crucial area if domestic concern which was hitherto the sole prerogative of the national government.

Trade Related Investment Measures

Among the new issues of negotiation where the

developing countries are to a large extent united are trade related investment measures. Since the conclusion of the Tokyo Round there have been attempts by developed countries, especially by the US, to bring issues of trade related investment measures under the GATT. The developing countries have resisted this attempt maintaining that the issue of foreign direct investment is beyond the jurisdictional competence of the GATT. It is argued by some that such measures have a clear trade impact.

Article III (Part-II) of the GATT contains the national treatment principle. Section 4 of this Article states: "The products of the territory of any contracting party imported into the territory of any other contracting party shall be accorded treatment no less favourable than that accorded to like products of national origin in respect of all laws, regulations and requirements affecting their internal sale, offering for sale, purchase, transportation, distribution, or use . . ." The developed countries have argued that for performance requirements — such as local content requirements, export obligations and other measures for foreign investor violate the national treatment provisions of the GATT by treating domestically produced goods more favourably than the imports. Similarly, the export performance requirements while not coming under Article 111 have definitely trade effects, argue developed countries. Hence, according to them investment measures pursued by the developing countries are subject to the GATT provision.

The foreign direct investment in developing countries have certain specific aspects which are of great concern to host developing countries.

First, it is considered that in a number of cases, the foreign investor does not come with adequate capital. What he does is to use local capital to finance his venture thus depriving local entrepreneurs and the government of the needed capital in a scarce capital situation. In fact, in the case of India, studies have proved that a number of foreign companies have not contributed more than 4 per cent of total capital from the overseas import.[27]

Second, it is also considered that a forcign investor would seek investment only in high profit-oriented sector.[28] This leads to two important effects: (i) High profit remittances; and (ii) deprivation of necessary capital to needy and priority sectors.

Third, the foreign investor will be more often interested in selling in the domestic market.[29] Thus, he would import more and export less or a negligible quantity. This situation once again leads to two important effects on the domestic economy of the host country. (a) There would be tremendous scope for transfer pricing leading to outflow of resources from host developing countries, and (b) balance of payments effects of this would be negative. There has been ample evidence on this. In the case of India, the balance of payments effects of operation of foreign investors has been negative. There is also evidence to show that these companies have indulged in transfer pricing.

Fourth, foreign direct investment, although it claims to bring in technology, has not cared to effect transfer of technology in host developing countries.

Finally, the ability of foreign direct investors, especially the large TNCs, have displayed substantial capacity to destabilise the governments of host countries.

Therefore, over the years, the developing countries have foreign direct investment policies which are meant to regulate the operation of foreign investors. These regulatory measures include a number of performance requirements. They are: (a) export obligation; (b) import restriction; (c) domestic production and purchase from domestic market of necessary products, and (d) restriction on employment of expatriates, etc. Some of these regulations apply exclusively to foreign investors.

The US and developed countries through trade related investment measures would like to prevent the regulation of foreign direct investment by the host developing countries and promote policies supporting capital exporting countries.

All developing countries are in agreement to propose a discipline limited to trade effects of TRIMS, if and when they are demonstrable. This puts the burden of proof on the complaining party rather than the party proposing TRIMS. Further, the mandate in Uruguay Round is very clear. "Following an examination of the operation of GATT Articles related to the trade restrictive and distorting effects of investment measures, negotiations should be elaborate as appropriate further provision that may be necessary to avoid such adverse effects of trade". Hence India had argued that it is not meant to extend the creation of "international investment regime".[30]

The Mid-Term Review of the Uruguay Round further reinforced the following:

(a) Further identification of the trade restrictive and distorting effects of investment measures that are, or may be, covered by existing GATT Articles, specifying those Articles;
(b) Identification of other trade restrictive and distorting effects of investment measures that may not be covered adequately by

existing GATT Articles, but are relevant to the mandate of the Group given by the Punta del Este Ministerial Declaration;

(c) Development aspects that would require consideration;

(d) Means of avoiding the identified adverse trade effects of trade related investment measures including, as appropriate, new provisions to be elaborated where existing GATT Articles may not cover them adequately; and

(e) Other relevant issues, such as the modalities of implementation.[31]

Despite this, the negotiations have proceeded on the basis of large and comprehensive TRIMS. This has primarily taken the form of a call for an investment regime and the elimination of TRIMS themselves rather than for minimizing and avoiding adverse effects of these measures.[32]

The performance requirements imposed by the host countries are normally in keeping with their priorities. These are prevalent in developed and developing countries; while in developed countries they are implicit, in developing countries they are explicit.[33]

Prohibition of TRIMS would circumscribe the capacity of host countries to align foreign investment with national priorities. A prohibition approach will have very high economic and development costs for most developing countries and any decision which circumscribes the capacity of governments to place conditionalities to investors without placing corresponding disciplines on the action of private operators would be unbalanced.[34]

It is important to note that a number of developed countries have sought to include in

TRIMS such issues as national treatment and transparency in a bid to make the foreign direct investment policies of host countries subject to discipline by an international agency. In one of its submissions to the Negotiating Group, Switzerland has proposed the consideration of TRIMS into three categories, namely, prohibited, permitted and actionable investment measures, while the United States has proposed consideration of the measures into two categories, namely, those that are prohibited in all circumstances because of their "inherently adverse trade effects" and those that are not prohibited in all circumstances, but should be subject to other disciplines under the GATT.[35] The United States has further proposed the elaboration of "illustrative lists" of TRIMS. The Indian presentation has argued that many of the developing countries think that the investment policies lie in the domain of national sovereign jurisdiction and domestic policy considerations are too vital for governments to allow a GATT Committee to sit on judgement over such policies or to decide whether a particular TRIM should be prohibited or otherwise actionable.[36]

It is significant that the Chairman of the negotiating group said on December 3, 1990: "Negotiations conducted in the relevant negotiating group have revealed that basic divergence of view continue to exist in respect of average level of discipline, additional flexibility to developing countries, discussion of restrictive business practices".

NOTES

1. Punta del Este Declaration.

2. South Commission, *Statement on the Uruguay Round*, P. 11.
3. Based on the assessment made by the Working Group of African Countries in UNCTAD.
4. Extracts of the Montreal Midterm Meeting, April 1989.
5. The Challenge to the South. p. 243.
6. Based on Draft Final Act of Uruguay Round, discussion with experts at Geneva, and Mid-term Review. Final Agreement statements made by representatives of a number of developing countries in Uruguay Round of Negotiations. See also, Ambassador Carla Hills' statement on textiles under Uruguay Round of Negotiations on 18th January, Discussion with Indian participants *Economic News From the United States* Jan-Feb 1991.
7. Diana Tasnadi, "Agriculture", *Business America*, Sept. 10, 1990.
8 Punta del Este Declaration. Rosine M. Plank, 'Proposals for Reforming GATT Rules and Disciplines on Agriculture in the Uruguay Round: Implications for and Needs of Developing Countries'. UN, *Uruguay Round Further Papers on Selected Issues* (UN, New York, 1990). Also see, Harmon Thomas, 'Agriculture in the Uruguay Round: Interests and Issues', *Uruguay Round Papers on Selected Issues* (UN, New York, 1989).
9. South Commission, *Statement on Uruguay Round*, P. 17.
10. These are the expectations as summarized by Rosine M. Plank, 'Proposals for reforming GATT Rules....' pp 49-51.
11. Bhagwati, J., 'Services' in J. Michael Finger and Andrez Olechowski (eds.), *The Uruguay Round* (World Bank Publication , Washington, 1987), Sumitra Chishti, 'Services and Economic Development of Developing Countries: Liberalization of International Trade in Services', *Indian Journal of Social Sciences*, vol. 2, no. 2, 1989.
12. The set was unanimously adopted by all States in General Assembly Resolution 3563 of 5 December, 1980.
13. For summary, see, review of these RBPS in Services. Philippe Brusick, Murray Gibbs and Mina Mashayekhi, 'Anti-Competitive Practices in the Services Sector', UN, *Uruguay Round Further Papers on Selected Issues* (UN, New York, 1990).

14. See for discussion of this subject, Sumitra Chishti, 'Services and Economic Development of Developing Countries Liberalization of International Trade in Services and its Impact', *Indian Journal of Social Science*, vol. 2, no.2. (1981)
15. South Commission, *Statement on Uruguay Round*, p. 21.
16. Punta del Este Declaration.
17. Louis J. Murray (Acting Director, Office of Multilateral Affairs, US Department of Commerce), 'Brussels Ministerial Inconclusive: GATT Talks Suspended to Allow Countries to Reflect on Position', *Economic News From the United States*, March, 1991.
18. *Ibid.*
19. Draft Final Act.
Assessment of the Results of the Uruguay Round from the Point of View of African Countries (Mimeographed). Evaluation on the situation of the Uruguay Round on behalf of SELA (Latin American Countries) since there was no united approach of Asia, there is no single report from Asian negotiators.
20. See for discussion, VanGrassteks Communication 'Trade Related Intellectual Property Rights, United States Trade Policy, Developing Countries and the Uruguay Round', UN, *Uruguay Round, Further Papers on Selected Issues* (UNCTAD, New York, 1990). 'Abdulquazi A. Yusuf, 'Developing Countries and Trade Related Aspects of Intellectual Property Rights', UN, *Uruguay Round Papers on Selected Issues* (UNCTAD, New York, 1989).
21. *Ibid.*
22. Louis Murphy, 'Uruguay Round Negotiations Overcome Stalemate', *Business America*, March 25, 1991.
23. India's presentation at GATT, July 12, 1989. *Document, Mainstream*, Aug 6, 1982.
24. Aan V. Deardroff, 'Should Patent Protection be Extended to all Developing Countries', (mimeographed), Nov. 8, 1990.
25. Based on statement made by the representatives in Geneva, 1990.
26. Statement by Dr. Subramaniam Swamy, Union Minister of Commerce, Law and Justice, Leader of Indian Delegation in Uruguay Round Ministerial Meeting in December 1990.

27. Sandip Choudhury, 'Financing Growth of Transnational Corporations in India 1976-77', *Economic and Political Weekly*, vol. XIV, no. 33, 18 August 1979 and Indian Institute of Foreign Trade, *The Role of Transnational Corporations in India's Exports* (IIFT, New Delhi, 1981), pp. 56-60.
28. N.S. Sidharthan, *Conglomerates and Multinationals in India* (Institute of Economic Growth, New Delhi, 1981). Louis Well Jr., 'Investment Incentives: an Unnecessary Debate', *The CTC Reporter*, no. 22, Autumn 1986.
29. Sanjaya Lal and Paul Streeten, *Foreign Investment Transnationals and Developing Countries* (Macmillan, London, 1977), pp. 130-140, 160-90. Reserve Bank of India, *Foreign Collaboration in Indian Industry* (Bombay, 1985). 'Finance of Public Limited Companies 1982-83, 1984-85' *Reserve Bank of India Bulletin*, May 1987.
30. India's stand on Trade Related Investment Measures as presented on August 5, 1989. Document reproduced. *Mainstream* 1989, Dec. 2.
31. Uruguay Round Mid-Term Review, *Focus*, May 1989.
32. Hardeep Puri and Delfino Bonded, 'TRIMS, Development Aspects and the General Agreement', UN, *Uruguay Round Further Papers on Selected Issues* (UNCTAD, 1990), p. 57.
33. Stephen Guisinger, *Investment Incentives and Performance Requirements* (Report of the World Bank, July 1983). IIFT, *Foreign Direct Investment in India, Malaysia and South Korea* (mimeographed).
34. Indian presentation.
35. Document MTN/GNG/NG 12/W/16. Document MTN/GNG/NG 12/W/15.
36. Based on presentation of India on September 14, 1989.

4

Issues of Organisational Restructuring under the Uruguay Round

The issue of organisational restructuring of world trade has been raised in the Uruguay Round of trade negotiations for the first time since the failure to establish international trade organisation in the forties and fifties. The group on Future of GATT System (FOGS) is cautious yet discussing the need to either reform the GATT or establish a new organisation. The reasons for it, as John H. Jackson puts it, are:

(1) The Uruguay Round is vast and complex and addresses several important 'new issues' particularly services, intellectual property rights and trade related investment measures. It is unclear how some of the results of negotiations on these issues can be incorporated into the GATT system. Thus a certain amount of thinking about the institutional structure will be necessary to prepare for the end of the Uruguay Round.

(2) There appears to be growing concern about the relationship between some of the Tokyo Round codes to the GATT system.

(3) The admittance of new or potential new

members (such as China) will require consideration of how the GATT system can embrace large economies structured on the basis of principles other than market economies.

(4) There is much concern about the dispute settlement process, and at least some recognition that the 'reforms' so far raised in the negotiations are relatively timid.

(5) Many other problems of the weak constitutional structure of the GATT system have been increasingly recognised.

(6) The world economy is changing at an increasingly rapid pace, and the GATT system is relatively rigid making it difficult to adapt it to many of the changes likely to occur. Thus it can be argued that a better 'constitution' will be needed for the next decade or next century, to address a large number of new issues.

(7) National governments recognise that an international structure of rules can be useful in seeking change at home.

(8) World economic relations have changed dramatically in recent decades. Changes include 'interdependence' and speed of communication, impact of economic circumstances on other countries, risky 'unilateral' actions by major trading nations, and the inability of the traditional GATT system rules effectively to address a series of new trading problems and structures".[1]

There have been a number of approaches to find either an alternative organisational set-up or widen the scope of functioning of the GATT as well as enhance the effectiveness of its decision-making, implementation and dispute settlement.

These approaches, as emanated from the discussion in the FOGS group as well as presentation of various representatives, can be classified into two major components: (i) Improving the GATT system as such; and (ii) establishing a new organisational set-up.

Improving the GATT System

The issue of improving the GATT system mainly refers to an enhanced surveillance in the GATT. The Ministers have recommended that the contracting parties confirm the establishment of the Trade Policy Review Mechanism. It is suggested that all contracting parties are subjected to periodic reviews and guidelines for such a review were expected to be finalised by June 1991. This was based on the hope of final negotiations being concluded by December 1990. This may now be postponed. Since there is little difference of opinion on this one can expect it to be completed immediately after the final negotiations are over. It is also suggested that after increased experience the review mechanism can be modified.

The Ministers also recommended that the domestic decision making must be more transparent. They confirmed the need for publication and notification of decision making of the governments of contracting parties.

The Ministers have also further stressed on the institutional reinforcement of the GATT which includes making a fuller contribution to the direction and content of the GATT system, reinforcement of the commitment of governments to the GATT system, giving greater prominence to the GATT in domestic policies, assessing trends in international trade and place these trends in their wider economic and political context, enabling contracting parties to contribute effectively to international discussion at the policy level of international adjustment process, and increasing the contribution of the GATT to a greater coherence in the global economic policy.

Many developing countries like India had expressed the view that the enhanced surveillance would not serve as a basis of enforcement of specific GATT obligations or dispute settlement procedures and would not require any new obligations in this respect. Furthermore, they felt that the process of the review of trade policies and practices is not intended to lead to conclusion or recommendations which may be of finding nature. Nor is it intended to establish the legal status of trade policies and practices. The process in their view should lead to an improved adherence to the rules and disciplines of the GATT and this should serve to strengthen the multilateral trading system. They were of the opinion that the enhancement of surveillance should concentrate on trade policies and practices of the major trading countries which have a predominant impact on the multilateral trading system. The principles with reference to which according to this presentation the monitoring has to take place will be necessarily those which are embodied in the General Agreement. This monitoring is expected to confine to trade policies and not to the economic policy framework. They also suggested a long-term frame for developing countries and in particular for the less developing among them.[2]

In fact, the surveillance of developing countries' policies has been widespread. As the South Commission puts it: "Under the rubric of 'Functioning of the GATT System' (FOGS) the

Uruguay Round includes negotiations about possible enhancement of the surveillance in the GATT as well as the possible strengthening of GATT's relationship with international monetary and financial organisations. On the first issue, it should be pointed out that developing countries are already subject to continuing surveillance under existing mechanisms, while developed countries are not, increased surveillance arrangements should therefore be directed primarily to the latter".[3]

The US is keen to change the decision-making structure of the GATT while it is cool to the establishment of a new organisation which will be discussed subsequently. Its proposal in the Negotiating Group on the functioning of the GATT emphasised that "Decision-making in the GATT has been hindered by the lack of an executive group within the organization".[4] The US believes that establishment within the GATT of the executive group at the Ministerial level is an essential element in improving the organization's overall effectiveness and decision-making.[5] This board will function to enable the GATT to function efficiently and also take the primary responsibility for developing an outline for the consideration by the contracting parties of a successor organization to the GATT (e.g., a World Trade Organization or Multilateral Trade Organization).

The proposal by the US is to consider the following elements, as formulated by its official spokespersons: The US believes that international organizations rely on small, representative groups of members to carry out certain functions that can not be carried out efficiently or in a timely fashion by the full membership. According to the US, drafters of the Havana Charter of the International Trade Organization (ITO) provided for a small, executive group within the organization, as did the charters of the Bretton Woods institutions.

The Punta del Este Ministerial Declaration calls for negotiations that:

Shall aim to develop understandings and arrangements. . . to improve the overall effectiveness and decision-making of the GATT as an institution, including, *inter alia*, through involvement of Ministers.

The United States believes that the establishment of a Management Board within the GATT, at the Ministerial level, is an essential element in improving the organization's overall effectiveness and decision-making.

According to its understanding, the contracting parties had agreed to meet regularly not less than every two years. As the body that would meet at the Ministerial level between the biennial plenary meetings of the contracting parties at Ministerial level, the Management Board is expected to be assigned other specific functions:

- to serve as a forum for discussion on trade issues of common concern and to resolve issues referred to it by the Council or taken up by the Board on its own initiative;
- to assist in the development of agendas and other preparations for the biennial plenary meetings of contracting parties at the Ministerial level, including decisions to initiate trade negotiations;
- to take primary responsibility for developing an outline, for consideration by the contracting parties, of a successor organization to the GATT (e.g., a World Trade Organization or a Multilateral Trade Organization);

- to serve as a nominating committee for the selection of the Director-General and Deputies Director-General; and
- to guide continuing co-operation between the GATT and the international financial institutions.

Relationship to Existing GATT Framework: The US envisages that as a management committee, the Management Board would have limited decision-making powers delegated to it by the contracting parties. It could deal with any issue assigned to it by the contracting parties, the Council of Representatives, or any other GATT bodies, or take up issues on its own. The contracting parties might assign to the Board issues where it has been difficult in the past to obtain a consensus within the Council of Representatives.

It is further considered that once the Management Board is established, the relationship of the functions of the Board and of the Consultative Group of Eighteen would need to be reviewed with a view toward eliminating duplication, the result of this review is likely to be the abolition of the Consultative Group of Eighteen.

It is expected that all contracting parties would be informed about the results of the deliberations of the Management Board. The Board could also issue press communiques or other statements following its meetings.

With regard to the size and the compositon of the Board the US proposal suggests that the Board shall consist of 18 members, distributed among contracting parties as follows:

- Four seats shall be reserved for contracting parties undergoing biennial review under the

Trade Policy Mechanism.

- Eight seats shall be reserved for contracting parties undergoing review under the Trade Policy Review Mechanism every four years, within this set of contracting parties, one-half would serve in alternative years.
- Six seats would be reserved for contracting parties undergoing review under the Trade Policy Review Mechanism every six years. Within this set of countries:
    - annual rotation shall be enforced; and
    - participation shall be representative of the broad geographic areas to which members belong.
- Only contracting parties that have fulfilled their TPRM obligations will be eligible for participation.

The Management Board is expected to meet as needed, but not less than twice a year. It would also meet in emergency sessions, if needed, to address matters of great urgency.

Establishing a New Organizational Set-up

In the later years of negotiations considerable thought has been given to the need to establish a new organizational set-up. This has been felt because of a number of agreements on various areas that have been covered under the Uruguay Round which do not confine to merchandise trade alone.

The Economic and Social Council in its 36th Plenary meeting on July 26, 1990 requested the Secretary-General to report to the General Assembly at its forty-sixth session, through the Economic and

Social Council at its second regular session of 1991, on institutional developments related to the strengthening of the international organization in the area of multilateral trade, taking into account the provisions of paragraph 32 of the Declaration on International Economic Cooperation, in particular revitalization of economic growth and development of the developing countries, adopted by the Assembly at its eighteenth special session.[6]

The Final Draft Act of the Uruguay Round provides for an administrative infrastructure for the international implementation of the Uruguay Round results. It is also considered desirable to establish a new multilateral trade organization or a new organizational structure which shall service GATT and start servicing the agreements. There are no details regarding the agreement in the draft Final Act. "The organizational agreement should include provisions on the establishment of a permanent institutional structure along the lines of the structure established for the negotiation".[7] There were also a number of suggestions outside Uruguay Round.

There are ideas like the one put forward by the Italian foreign trade minister suggesting transforming the GATT into a full-fledged international trade organization with regulatory power and close links with the IMF and the World Bank. The Canadian representative presented Canada's proposal for a world trade organization. EEC formally submitted in the FOGS negotiating group a proposal for the establishment of a Multilateral Trade Organization. In October 1990, the US made a formal submission to the FOGS negotiating group on the establishment of a GATT management board which has already been discussed.

The main elements of Canadian and EEC's proposals are presented below. The Canadian proposal emphasized that since there have been large-scale changes in international trade and economic environment, the need to establish a new institutional framework which is expected to provide a 'credible' multilateral alternative to unilateral action. The reason offered for this is that the GATT has become unwieldy since it has become a large arrangement consisting of 97 countries of which a large number of them are developing countries. While the dispute settlement of the GATT has been effective, it is considered not effective enough to provide a credible integrated mechanism for the resolution of trade disputes. The world trade organisation would be, therefore, expected to provide a solution while it will focus its attention on implementing the substantive understanding under the Uruguay Round.

The broad thrust of the Canadian proposal is to provide an institutional character to the GATT. Its official position on this issue is as follows:

"*World Trade Organisation (WTO)* : Developments in the substantive negotiations are now demonstrating that the Uruguay Round results cannot be effectively housed in a provisional shelter. It is also becoming clear that the post-Uruguay Round trade policy agenda will be complex and may not be adequately managed within the confines of the GATT system as it now exists."

Canada proposed that it would come forward with a draft of an umbrella framework around the time of the July TNC (1990) when the profile of the overall, substantive MTN package should have emerged from the detailed negotiations in the various negotiations in the various negotiating groups.

According to Canada "The draft could provide a basis for examination through the fall of how the results of the Round could be incorporated into a new institutional structure. As part of a major and substantive result in the Uruguay Round, Ministers would decide in Brussels to create a World Trade Organisation. Detailed administrative arrangements could be worked out in early 1991".

According to the proposed new organizational set-up by Canada, the substantive obligations of the GATT, other existing agreements and the Uruguay Round agreements would not be changed. The WTO would provide an institutional framework and formal legal status for the overall, multilateral trading system. It should be approved by the national legislative authorities as part of the approvals necessary to implement the overall, MTN trade agreements.

A major contribution of a new WTO is expected to provide the institutional capacity and credibility for the new GATT trading system to engage in more sustained and effective cooperation with the IMF and the IBRD. Indeed, it is argued that the key to increased economic policy coherence lies in a successful MTN which would result in improved and expanded trade rules, an effective dispute settlement system and increased transparency in the development of national trade policies and practices.

Further, it is stated: "In recognition of the need for increased coherence between monetary, trade and financial policies, governments should also agree on a number of concrete initiatives to be taken to enhance cooperation with the IMF and the IBRD."

The EEC's proposal for Multilateral Trade Organisation has been very comprehensive. The main elements of the proposal are listed below:

Establishment: The Multilateral Trade

organisation is expected to be established to further the achievement of the purposes of the General Agreement on Trade in Goods, the Uruguay Round Agreements on Trade in Goods, (the Agreement of TRIPS) and the General Agreement on Services.

Regarding the membership, the EEC's proposal suggests that members of the MTO shall be the contracting parties to the Multilateral Trade Agreements.

Further, the EEC's proposal expects that the MTO shall administer the Multilateral Trade Agreements as well as any other multilateral trade agreement negotiated under the auspices of GATT or the MTO and generally facilitate their operation;

The MTO shall have authority to take appropriate actions to facilitate the operation and further the objectives of the Multilateral Trade Agreements subject to the limitations specified in these agreements;

In particular, the MTO

(i) shall adopt and administer an integrated dispute settlement mechanism; and
(ii) shall adopt and administer a Trade Policy Review Mechanism;

The MTO may also launch negotiations in areas relevant to the purposes of the Multilateral Trade Agreements;

Further, that no decision or other action of the MTO shall have the effect of imposing on a Member any new substantive obligations which the Member has not specifically agreed to undertake.

The structure of MTO as envisaged in the EEC proposal is as follows:

The MTO shall have a General Council, a Goods

Council, (a TRIPS Council) and a Services Council.

General Council: The General Council shall consist of the Members of the MTO. It shall carry out the functions of the MTO. It may establish subsidiary bodies. It shall establish its own rules of procedure and shall approve rules of procedure of the Goods Council, (the TRIPS Council), the Services Council and any subsidiary body.

The Goods Council: The Goods Council shall exercise the functions of contracting parties of the General Agreement of Tariffs and Trade and of the Uruguay Round Agreements on Trade in Goods. (Similar arrangement is envisaged for other agreements on TRIP and TRIM).

The Services Council: The Services Council shall exercise the functions of the parties of the General Agreement on Trade in Services.

The Secretariat is expected to consist of the following:

(a) Director-General as chief administrative officer of the MTO appointed by the General Council. The powers, duties, conditions of service and term of office of the Director-General will be confirmed by the regulations approved by the General Council.

(b) He or his representative shall be entitled to participate, without the right to vote, in all meetings of the General Council and subsidiary bodies of the MTO.

(c) The Director-General would appoint the members of the staff, and fix their duties and conditions of service in accordance with regulations approved by the General

Council.

(d) The responsibilities of the Director-General and of the members of the staff are exclusively international in character. In the discharge of their duties, they are not to seek or receive instructions from any government or from any other authority external to the MTO. They are expected to refrain from any action which might reflect on their positions as international officials. The Members shall respect the international character of the responsibilities of these persons and shall not seek to influence them in the discharge of their duties.

Each member of the MTO shall be entitled to have one vote and, except as otherwise provided for in this Agreement and the Multilateral Trade Agreements, decisions of the General Council shall be taken by a majority of the vote cast. The General Council shall endeavour to decide on the basis of consensus.

Budget and Contributions:

The Director-General shall be the authority to present to the General Council the annual budget estimates and financial statement of the MTO. The General Council shall approve the accounts and the budget.

The General Council would fbe having the authority to apportion the expenditures of the MTO among the Members in accordance with a scale of contributions to be fixed by the Council, and each Member would contribute promptly to MTO its share of these expenditures.

If a Member is in arrears in the payment of its contributions by an amount which equals or exceeds the amount of contributions due from it in respect of the preceding two completed financial years, the Member would cease to have a vote, and would not be counted in the determining of the fulfilment of the relevant voting requirements, in the organs of the MTO. If the General Council is satisfied that the failure to pay is due to circumstances beyond the control of the Member, it may, nevertheless, permit such a Member to vote, and then such Member shall be counted accordingly.

The MTO would be a legal personality which will enjoy in the territory of each of the Members such legal capacity, privileges and immunities as may be necessary for the exercise of its functions.

The representatives of the Members and the officials of the MTO shall enjoy such privileges and immunities as may be necessary for the independent exercise of their functions in connection with the MTO.

The privileges and immunities to be accorded by a Member to the MTO, to its officials and to the representatives of its Members would be similar to those accorded by that Member to specialised agencies of the United Nations, to their officials and to the representatives of their members, under the Convention of the Privileges and Immunities of the Specialised Agencies, or under similar arrangements.

The MTO is expected to make arrangements with

intergovernmental bodies and agencies which have related responsibilities to provide for effective cooperation and the avoidance of unnecessary duplication of activities.

According to the proposal, the MTO may make suitable arrangements for consultation and cooperation with non-governmental organisations concerned with matters within the scope of the MTO and, decisions of amendments of this Agreement would be taken by two-thirds of the Members.

These approaches have obviously led to a discussion, especially in view of reference to the ill fated International Trade organisation (ITO). Therefore, it is useful to recall the main elements of ITO which were relevant from the point of view of developing countries.

The GATT was carved out of ITO. But there were important chapters in the non-ratified ITO charter, which are important specially from the point of view of developing countries.

Chapter II at the Havana Charter on "*Employment and Economic Activity*" saw full employment not as merely a domestic objective but a matter of common responsibility. This was because of the fact that the great depression of the thirties had created huge unemployment. Providing full employment had became the objective of all major counties. Members would therefore be obliged to take action designed to achieve and maintain full and productive employment and large and steadily growing demand within their territories. They were also to enter into arrangements to exchange information on domestic employment problems, national income demand etc. and the ITO would have been empowered to initiate consultations among members with a view to their taking appropriate measures against the international spread of a decline in employment, production or demand. In addition, Members recognised the need to take fully into account the rights of workers under intergovernmental declarations, conventions and agreements. It was also envisaged that all matters relating to labour standards would be taken up by the ITO in consultation and cooperation with the International Labour Organisation.

On "*Economic Development and Reconstruction*", ITO charter in its chapter III, recognised the importance of the industrial and general economic development of all countries, particularly of those in which resources are as yet relatively underdeveloped, and states that "the productive use of the world human and material resources is of concern to and will benefit all countries". It noted that development requires "adequate supplies of capital funds, materials, modern equipment and technology and technical and managerial skills" and called for cooperation among members to stimulate and assist in the provision and exchange of these facilities. Provision was made for technical assistance by the ITO, which would also "make recommendations and promote agreements designed to facilitate an equitable distribution of skills, arts, technology, material and equipment with due regard to needs of all members" (Article 11.2(b)) and "formulate and promote the adoption of a general agreement or statement of principles regarding the conduct, practices and treatment of foreign investment" (Article 11.2(c)). Certain principles regarding the latter area are put forward in Article 12, which reflects some of the views of the developing countries while in exchange providing for safeguards against "mistreatment of foreign investors" involving in the last instance the International Court of Justice.

This chapter, therefore, touched upon a variety of issues that are of crucial preoccupation today, and where efforts were being made to establish effective international disciplines. These include, in particular, negotiations of the Codes of Conduct on the Transfer of Technology, and on Transnational Corporations.

Chapter V on "*Restrictive Business Practices*" contained definitions of RBPs, envisaged consultation and investigation procedures among Members, as well as general obligations to avoid such practices. Special procedures were elaborated regarding RBPs in Services, such as transportation, telecommunications, insurance and the commercial services of banks.

The ITO gave importance to commodity problems and recognized the need for intergovernmental action. Therefore, in Chapter VI on "*Intergovernmental Commodity Agreements*" it was recognised that production and trade in primary commodities may be affected by a tendency of persistent disequilibrium between production and consumption, the accumulation of burdensome stocks and pronounced fluctuations in prices. The objective of price stabilisation and the need for economic adjustment was stressed and reference was made to the protection of the natural resources of the world from "unnecessary exhaustion" and to the equitable distribution of primary commodities in short supply. Special attention was given to commodity control agreements, defined as involving (a) the regulation of production or the quantitative control of exports and imports, or (b) the regulation of prices. Agreements of this type were made subject to certain requirements, which would confine them to certain agricultural staples (fulfilling conditions such as actual or expected surpluses and small producers accounting for a substantial part of total output) and mineral products in isolated communities (fulfilling such conditions as actual or expected unemployment causing or threatening to cause serious hardship and the absence of alternative employment in the areas concerned). In brief, while recognising the particular commodity issues, the operational provisions are restrictive in nature, representing a compromise which might have been difficult to operate in practice.

Chapter VII of the ITO Charter provided for the establishment of the International Trade Organisation (ITO), and Chapter VIII for the settlement of differences within its auspices. The ITO was intended to be a very active organisation, concerned with virtually all issues in the areas of trade, employment, and development and, in general, the management of the world economy. The institutional aspects of the ITO covered such subjects as: membership; functions; bodies (Conference, Executive Board, Commissions, Director-General and Staff) and their rules of procedure; relations with the United Nations and other international organisations; international legal status; contributions.[8]

Attempts have been made over the years to achieve the objective of some chapters of ITO through various unorganizations. The objective of UNCTAD and the UNCTC are partly to draw their sustenance from this. In this context the EEC proposal on the MTO appears to be very narrow in scope, far away from the philosophy and provisions of the Havana Charter. Consideration is only being given in the MTO proposal to the institutional framework of the GATT with a view to ensuring "pragmatically" implementation of the results of the Uruguay Round, especially as regards incorporation of the results on Services, TRIPS and TRIMS. So the original idea of the ITO, as envisaged by the Havana Charter, is only being invoked in form and not in substance. In reality, the EEC considers incorporating only those features of the evolving multilateral trading system which respond to the growing ambitions of the industrialised countries without any reference to the preoccupations of developing countries.

The specific elements of the EEC proposal, though institutional in form, contain significant dangers and adverse implications for developing countries. It is clear that there are intentions to create under an umbrella of an MTO a solid basis for inclusion of the Uruguay Round results on services, TRIPS and TRIMS into multilateral trading system and existing GATT related disciplines on trade in goods and at the same time to adopt unique dispute settlement procedures applying to "all relevant multilateral instruments" within the system. Once this is accomplished, it would be possible to undertake cross-sectoral retaliation, it is felt.

The senior trade officials' meeting on Uruguay Round of some developing countries, held in New Delhi in March 1990, is believed to have clearly opposed the proposal to establish results in the new areas of negotiations (TRIPS, TRIMS and Services) into the GATT with cross sectoral linkages with goods.[9]

These proposals have also included the need for increased cooperation between MTO, IMF and the World Bank as was stated by the Italian representative. There has been a proposal by Mexico to establish a link between trade, monetary and financial issues. It has been stated in its presentation : "There is a clear need for the international community to tackle the problems arising from the trade/money/finance/debt nexus in the comprehensive manner, in order to progress towards the establishment of a more equitable and efficient international economic system that can promote sustained growth of the world economy and renewed economic development of developing world."[10]

The GATT, the IMF and the World Bank, each has its own mandate, and differs substantially in structure and resources. Nevertheless, it is perceived that their concerns increasingly overlap and this trend is reinforced by the increasing need for the GATT to deal with non-border measures and policies, and new areas of trade. Two approaches have been identified. One aims at an informal relationship between the GATT on one side and Bretton Woods institution on the other. The other approach is based on the belief that the present information is insufficient and must lead to a formal agreement on institutional cooperation. There are pressures to accept the latter approach.

Collaboration with the IMF and the World Bank is one of the main elements of the new organisational restructuring, i.e., to establish close formal contact between the GATT or the new agencies and the IMF and the World Bank. This would bring all developing countries under one policy framework where three international institutions will dictate developing countries regarding their international and internal economic policies. This will also lead to a type of application of cross conditionality which has been the result of the IMF and the World Bank loans under their various lending arrangements. This may be linked with the administration of various arrangements in the Uruguay Round. Thus the developing countries would enter into a highly complex interrelated trading, financial and monetary arrangement in the World system which they can handle only when they fully accept it. Even so, some developing countries for want of special knowledge may fail to cope with it and thus may be led down the garden path by the developed countries.

Negotiations Strategy under Uruguay Round and its Implications

It may be noted that the Uruguay Round of Multilateral Trade Negotiations has been the most 'ambitious' programme of negotiation because not only merchandise trade negotiation but also various non-trade sectors such as trade related intellectual property rights, trade related investment measures and also liberalisation of trade in services have been included in its purview. A large number of developing countries are not capable of fully comprehending the implications of the negotiations under these heads.

In the Uruguay Round the emphasis has been on accepting the package as a single undertaking. "The launching, the conduct and the implementation of outcome of the negotiations shall be treated as part of a single understanding".[11] The choice for the developing countries in this respect has been difficult. Either they submit themselves totally to the agreement or they may not be allowed to become a party to those parts of the Agreement which they accept.

If a country is unable to accept such a single protocol, it would be asked to withdraw from the GATT. It may be recalled that para 2 of GATT's Article XXX states: "The contracting parties may decide that any amendment made effective under this Article is of such a nature that the contracting party which has not accepted it within a period specified by the contracting parties shall be free to withdraw from this Agreement, or to remain a contracting party with the consent of contracting parties". Alternately, it has been conceived that the countries accepting the single protocol incorporating the existing GATT and the results of the Round would withdraw from the GATT under Article XXXI and proceed to form a new integrated trade agreement. Such a possibility has been mentioned "as a leverage to achieve a desirable balance of rights and obligations". This is also expected to prevent a 'Cafeteria approach' or an 'a la carte approach' as in the Tokyo Round.

The single undertaking which has been the basis of this approach has been with regard to goods as stated in the Punta del Este Declaration. The linking with the other agreement was not the intention. Now the term 'global undertaking' has been used as being synonymous with 'single undertaking'.

The decision about the goods getting clubbed with other areas as a part of a single protocol would have the effect of making the benefits of market access negotiation conditional upon access to the entire package of results.

The Uruguay Round finalisation provides a challenging legal question to incorporate TRIMS Services, TRIPS as well as Codes in a single Protocol. The developing countries are concerned about the following elements in any of the new international trade organisational structure. It is feared by a number of developing countries that the new institutional mechanism expects to legitimise what they term as "cross retaliation", i.e., bounded concessions could be withdrawn in retaliation for the actions taken by the developing countries in respect of services and intellectual property rights.

The single protocol approach also proposed with an intention of preventing a continued drift to 'conditional MFN' exacerberates this situation as it would imply that developing countries not prepared to accept every element of the Uruguay Round would not benefit from any of the concessions and in addition might find themselves excluded from the new institution. This is true of a smaller developing country which had no opportunity to effectively take part in most areas of the negotiations and fear excluded by what they term forced 'globality'. If a developing country expels a bank or does not give landing rights to an airline of a country that country can withdraw concessions on garments or fruit juice.

'Cross-retaliation' has been legitimised in the US Trade Act: In order to avoid this sort of unilateralism, the retaliation is expected to be multilateralised. The view that in order to discipline the US this is necessary is not considered to be valid. The US will be happy that the principle of cross retaliation has been accepted multilaterally.

The umbrella type organisation will make UNCTAD more and more ineffective. The new organisation is not expected to have any relationship with the UN since it has not been contemplated in any proposal. Neither the General Assembly nor ECOSOC will have any powers to scrutinise the new organisation. Thus the MTO or WTO as envisaged are far away from an International Trade Organisation which can also serve the interest of developing countries.

NOTES

1. John H. Jackson, *Restructuring of GATT*, pp. 91-92.

2. Based on the Draft Final Act and presentations of India and other developing countries in the FOGS Group.
3. South Commission, *Uruguay Round*, p. 15
4. Proposal by the United States in Negotiating Group on the Functioning of the GATT System, MTN.GNG/NGIG/W/45.
5. *Ibid.*
6. Economic and Social Council T/1990/IMF/8, August 15, 1990.
7. Draft *Final Plan* Act.
8. Based on proceedings of the UNCTAD seminar on Restructing of International Trade Organization in 1990 *See*, Richard N. Gardner and Max F. Mihkan (ed) *The Global Partnership* (Scientific Book Agency, Calcutta, 1969); Robert E. Asher, Walter M. Kotshony *et al*, *United Nations and Economic and Social Cooperation*, (The Brooking Institutions, Wisconsin, 1957).
9. First Ever Meeting of the Senior Officials of Developing Countries held in third week of March 1990, in New Delhi, *Business Standard*, March 22, 1990; Discussion with UNCTAD officials.
10. Proposal by the Delegation of Mexico.
11. Ministerial Declaration on the Uruguay Round, GATT, *Focus*.

5

Dilemma of Developing Countries in the Nineties and Beyond

One can envisage that the developing countries will be expected in the nineties to confront a world trading system in which the rules governing their relationship with the rest of the world would have undergone substantial alteration. It will be useful to enumerate these new/altered rules which will steadily enter into the world trading system.

(i) The developing countries cannot expect that they would be continuously accorded preferential treatment in recognition of their special problems. The serious application of the graduation principle as defined by the developed countries would remove a large number of developing countries from the list of beneficiaries enjoying special and differential treatment.

(ii) Reciprocity will become increasingly an integral part of international negotiations: not only first degree reciprocity but also aspects of end result reciprocity. Negotiations based on the non-reciprocal principle may be a thing of past.

(iii) The issue of national treatment in sectors

such as services and foreign investment wherever necessary, would become increasingly dominant. This concept of national treatment would reduce the choices available to developing countries in framing their economic policies protecting their national interest.

(iv) Transparency in all policy measures of the developing countries as defined by the developed countries shall be increasingly dominating the policy making of developing countires.

(v) There would be increasing cooperation between the IMF and the World Bank on the one hand and the GATT or the new world trade organization on the other, in directing the economic policies of developing counties.

Where do the developing countries stand now, and what has happened to their effort to reorder world trading system consistent with their needs under the MTN negotiations? The results of various developments leading to effective negotiations in the Uruguay Round have finally re-established the primacy of the objectives of developed countries with a powerful movement towards the reversal of all concepts, principles and measures that were to come into effect progressively in the world trading system. It is important to highlight these developments as it is necessary to understand them as different from those principles which have been talked about over the last decades. The main thrust of these ideas was to provide developing countries a choice. But under the principle and rules of international relations they will be forced to integrate selectively into the world economic system not so much by their choice, as by the economic forces that these developments would unleash and strengthen. The developing countries would find themselves totally fragmented in the world economic system and aligned to a specific developed country in particular and the developed countries in general.

The first casualty of this has been the principle of collective bargaining. While it was only an optimist who could believe in the total fruitfulness of collective bargaining, there was, however, some hope. But the developments and the negotiations in the Uruguay Round finally laid to rest the collective bargaining as a concept, as a bargaining tool of the developing countries.

The concept of non-reciprocal arrangements wherein the developing countries were expected to be free from offering concessions in return to what they got is also under considerable strain. It must be stated that while the results of this approach have been exaggerated, as a concept it survived in the international negotiations providing some scope for independent action by the developing countries. The effective offers under the Uruguay Round seem to link the developing countries explicitly or implicitly to reciprocity although the Punta del Este declaration had committed to non-reciprocal aspect of negotiations.

Yet another principle detrimental to the unity of developing countries is the principle of selectivity. There has been an endeavour to legitimise the principle of selectivity in the GATT system thus introducing the principle of penalty to an 'erring' and 'deviant' developing country.

The inclusion of trade related intellectual property rights and trade related investment measures in the MTN has brought to focus a very important issue, i.e., the status of domestic economic sovereignty of developing countries. The scope and the direction of these agreements are very clear on one point: the domestic economic measures taken by a sovereign developing country are subject not only to investigation but also reformulation by an international body dominated by the developed countries. Further, if these measures are either found inconsistent or perceived as inconsistent with the expectations of the developed countries, they are expected to be abandoned regardless of their role in the domestic economy of the concerned developing country. This development must be seen along with the conditionality principle affecting the macroeconomic policies of developing countries borrowing from the multilateral institutions such as the IMF and the World Bank. Even the regional banks, such as the Asian Development Bank insist on 'conditionality' while lending to a developing country. Thus, we are entering an era in which the economic sovereignty of developing countries will be seriously eroded.

The decision making power in the economic institutions like the IMF and the World Bank has always been with the developed countries and dominated by the US. But there was some power in the GATT system with contracting developing countries to assert their way while in the UN they had a majority vote enabling them to assert their viewpoint. But this was in a way only notional. The decisions undertaken on the basis of majority vote in the UN system, such as in the UNCTAD, hardly got implemented if they were opposed by the developed countries. The same has been true in the GATT system. Very often waivers were sought to overcome the GATT discipline. Yet there was a legal position of importance to developing countries. Under the suggested restructuring of the trade organization, this legal position will be replaced by various types of voting in which the developed countries will have the final say.

Another major development which will make the developing countries 'captive countries' is the building in of the principle of 'cross retaliation' in the dispute settlement mechanism. If a country is found not behaving in accordance with the specific understanding under the MTO in a concerned field the complaining country can legitimately introduce 'cross retaliation' in an area of great significance to the so called deviant country. This is considered as a dangerous development affecting all aspects of policies of developing countries.

The principle of reciprocity is no longer confined to general agreement on reciprocal concessions. It is now linked with the end results. The results of reciprocity are important to assess the status of reciprocity as agreed to in various concessions. This again makes the vulnerable nations devise ways and means by which results are achieved that may be inconsistent with their needs.

Another important component of international economic relations is the emergence of unilateralism. In fact, the US is in a mood to pursue unilateralism to achieve its economic objectives if the multilateral trading arrangements do not suit it. If the Uruguay Round does not conclude successfully, it is very likely the world would witness tremendous growth of unilateralism and bilateralism. The developing counties ought to consider this possibility seriously.

The major question now confronting the developing countries, therefore, is what exactly should be their response to such a world economic system. It is important to recognise that old concepts and old strategies have outlived their utility. They must be abandoned and new concepts and new strategies recognizing the changed reality must replace them. What could be the core of this approach?

It is necessary to understand whether the hopes and planning strategy of the South, or the developing countries, are consistent with the changing interests of developing countries as they are perceiving them in the context of various developments that have taken place and are taking place. One finds that there is belief that the South would come together while dealing with the North as well as ensure collective self-reliance. The expectations are based on the assumption that the North-South relationship must be based on "shared benefits". This has been very well articulated by the South Commission in its Report. "The central message of this Report is that, to get ahead, the South must primarily rely on itself". This implies that the South should make efforts to overcome its underdevelopment through its own endeavour.

Further, it is argued by the South Commission: "But this message should not obscure the reality that the possibility of development in the South is closely tied to an improvement in its relationship with the North. The South needs the North as a market for its exports, as supplier of essential imports for consumption and production, as a source of technology and of capital. Additionally, the South requires more cooperation from the North for its efforts to achieve self-reliance. Collective self-reliance is not autarky. It does not mean opting out of economic relations with the North. Scientific and technological innovations - originating mostly in the North - is opening up undreamt of possibilities for human progress, the spread of global relations is a source of economic, social and political dynamism. *The issue for the South is not whether to cut its links with the North, but how to transform them* (italics added). The relationship must be changed from exploitation to shared benefit, from subordination to partnership. We believe this is a feasible objective because the North also needs the South".

This hope is based on three major assumptions. *First*, the North needs the South. *Second*, there is a collective will of the South. And, *third*, there is an identity of needs. All these assumptions are based either on an inadequate appreciation of the reality as evolving or because of willingly overlooking of the reality which is extremely painful to the proponents of 'collective South'. The latter aspect seems to be nearer the truth.

Let us examine the first assumption that the North also needs the South. The basis of need as understood can be classified into two groups: (a) the social tensions that are there in the South and (b) the prospects of the growth of these tensions would affect the stability of the North. This is true. But it would be so in the long run. The North has enough military and other power to quell the tensions which would undermine its stability. Any challenge which has in it instability of the North would be wiped out. We have witnessed in the latest case of the Gulf crisis that the supply and price of oil — one of the most important elements of the economic stability of the North — has been handled with unprecedented cooperation among the countries of the North under the leadership of the US. Hence, it is difficult to accept the proposition that the North would be deeply concerned about the social tensions of the South and help the South in a substantial way to overcome this tension. Further, apart from military strength, the North also has the necessary economic instruments to contain the tensions in such a manner that they will not basically undermine the stability of the North. This may be through fragmentation of the South. 'Collective South' is not on its agenda of cooperation. It would like to deal individually and at best in groups. This has been very well proved in the Uruguay Round and also by the bilateral approaches of the US, EEC and Japan.

The South Commission argues as follows: "The North also needs the South for good economic reasons. Developing countries have become increasingly important in the world economy. Before the onset of the crisis of the 1980s, they accounted for over one-fifth of global GDP, a share comparable to that of the EC. Their weight as export markets had grown accordingly; by that time they were taking about one-fourth of the total exports of the developed countries. They provided a market for nearly 40 per cent of US exports, and for half of Japan's. Recovery and sustained development in the South will therefore enlarge the demand for the North's exports — to the North's advantage. Faster growth in the South will spur international flows of trade and investment, faster growth and employment in the North, and help to reduce payments imbalances among industrial countries.

"The weight of the South in the world economy was demonstrated by the crisis of the 1980s, which caused it to reduce its imports sharply, leading to a substantial diminution of its role as a market for exports from developed countries. Had the South's ability to import in 1984-87 been at the same proportionate level as in 1981-83, the South's purchases from the North would have totalled nearly $1500 billion; in the event, because of the crisis and the contraction of imports, they fell below $1200 billion. The cumulative loss in exports to the industrialised world in those four years was more than the value of whole year's global exports of the United States.

"The resumption of development in the South is equally important in another area of central interest to the developed world: the protection of the global environment. Poverty is a major degrader of the habitat, and the state of the environment in the South is of critical importance to the health of the global ecology. Thus, the promotion of sustainable development in the South is demonstrably in the interest of the North as well, a point by now increasingly recognized by the influential environmental lobby in the North".[1]

Here again, the North would get its needs filled by bilateral relations and relations through international economic institutions. The bahaviour of the US has reiterated the approach, i.e., using the market access power to enable the countries of the South to behave as it wants. The policy dialogue and policy reform suggested by the IMF and the World Bank would have created and would create conditions which would meet the needs of the North without much difficulty.

The acceptance of interdependence by the negotiators of the South is not a new one. This has been the basis of many strategies of economic cooperation in the past. Let us now see how international cooperation can be strengthened. The old concept of interdependence needs to be looked into in order to find out whether it has the potential of providing an adequate political and economic base for a new era of international economic cooperation. The burden of the song so far as the old concept of interdependence is concerned is economic. The New International Economic Order is expected to be built on a number of basic concepts, including, especially, interdependence. The Brandt Commission states:

"The issue today is not only, or even mainly, one of and rather of basic changes in the world economy to help (the) developing countries pay their own way. And the countries of the North, given their increasing interdependence with the South, themselves and international economic reforms to ensure their own future prosperity".[2]

The UNCTAD VI launched negotiations on the basis of the premise that the developing countries were important to the developed countries in so far as they provided the necessary markets for their exports and increased employment opportunities and were sources of raw materials. As is well known, it met with failure.

While the developed countries need the developing countries, it is clear that their dependence on the developing countries is exaggerated. First, technological developments have increasingly enabled the developed countries to depend on themselves individually and as a group. Second, there is a conscious effort among the developed countries at the national, regional, and global levels to promote collaboration between and among themselves. This development can be seen in the efforts for the emergence of an integrated Europe in 1992, the formation of Group 7 to design international policies, and the flow of direct foreign investment. In the 1980s only a few developing countries received any large flow of direct investment. On the other hand the United States was the largest recipient of the flow of direct investment in 1986 (about 40 per cent of the total). The Soviet Union and the erstwhile socialist countries may support this tendency partly by joining international organisations and partly by withdrawing their support for the various proposals made by the developing countries. Third, the TNCs, the powerful agents of finance, trade, and industrial manufactures, do not depend on this approach in their attempts to globalize their production, distribution and marketing. With the help of various corporate strategies and support from the governments of the countries of their parent companies and international economic institutions they can achieve their objectives without taking recourse to these concepts and policies.

It is important to know whether this old concept of interdependence has any potential for providing the necessary impetus for the North to abandon its present strategy of going it alone in international affairs irrespective of whether the South as a group joins or not. The North is sure that a divided South would join.

The concept of 'Collective South' based on an identity of needs has also changed. Once the role of international market in the economic development of developing countries is given primacy, the collective effort to redirect the forces that have been generated by the market forces do not come into existence. The identity of interest attribute may not really exist in the context of the developing countries. Their perception of the needs and the assessment of strategies may vary.

With the collapse of collective bargaining another accompanying element of developing countries, i.e., South-South cooperation, has also faced difficulty. South-South cooperation, has never been an effective alternative/substitute programme. This was for a number of reasons. *First*, the capacity or potential of developing countries is not large enough to even remotely provide an alternative. In fact, all efforts towards regional cooperation among developing countries have not succeeded partly because of political reasons and partly because of their inadequate potential, since their trade and financial relations with the rest of the world are large and growing while their mutual relations have been stagnating and even declining. *Second,* owing to the fact of the early stages of their development - economic and political - these countries do not have the political will to forge a relationship amongst themselves overlooking their immediate and short-term problems. *Third,* especially with the collapse of the Socialist system, the domination of the developing countries by the developed countries has become more glaring and explicit. Any endeavour which will affect even marginally their interest, would interfere with their economic strategy and they would endeavour to prevent it from blooming.

The dilemma of developing countries in this evolving international economic order has been and will be as to how to adjust with the system and minimize the possible adverse effects as well as loss of sovereignty in economic decision making to which they are not willing participants. One can visualize some alternative scenarios.

In the first scenario, which is the most probable one, each developing country will pursue policies which will integrate it in the world economic system without any significant options open to it to modify its integration process consistent with the national perception of its needs. This may result in considerable suffering to weaker sections of the population, loss of gains from international trade and, in fact, inadequate growth of a large number of vital sectors which need the support of the State initially. For, history has shown that total reliance on market forces, national and international, does affect the poor adversely. The poor will be poor within a national system and the poor countries globally.

The second scenario is that a group of countries in a region try to cooperate and coordinate their policies towards integration with the world economy. This may reduce the adverse effects on them while providing some options to manage international economic relations at least to a certain extent consistent with their national perception. But the chances of successful regional cooperation among developing countries are not very bright. The history of their efforts towards regional economic cooperation shows that there are few integrating factors while factors working against the integration are very strong. The experiments in ASEAN, SAARC have not included the economic integration as a primary objective while the only successful attempt at integration, i.e., European Community, had right from the beginning aimed at the economic integration as the primary objective and a necessary first step.

The third scenario, i.e., all the developing countries joining together in a pursuit of collective approach, is the least likely scenario as has already been seen.

It is, therefore, important to take recourse to new methods. A number of developing countries have failed in this test. While international support is important, domestic effort recognizing domestic needs will alleviate the misery of the developing countries to a large extent.

Exaggerated expectations from the international community to assist developing countries unnecessarily divert their attention from the necessity of taking hard decisions at home.

NOTES

1. The Challenge to the South, The Report of the South Commission (Oxford Publishing House, Oxford, 1990), p. 5. Italics are added.
2. *North-South: A Programme of Survival:* Report of the Independent Commission on International Development Issues under the Chairmanship of Willy Brandt (London, 1980), p. 33.
3. Gamani Corea, 'Problem and prospect of UNCTAD VI" *Foreign Trade Review* (New Delhi), *Vol. 17, pp. 154-55.*

APPENDICES

The items included in the Appendices trace chronologically various provisions and decisions taken by the international community in the international economic institutions and the UN to build a world trading system in which the needs of the developing countries are given a special status and accorded a differential treatment. They also include the Punta del Este Declaration.

APPENDIX I

General Agreement on Tariffs and Trade

Article I

General Most-Favoured-Nation Treatment

1. With respect to customs duties and charges of any kind imposed on or in connection with importation or exportation or imposed on the international transfer of payments for imports or exports, and with respect to the method of levying such duties and charges, and with respect to all rules and formalities in connection with importation and exportation, and with respect to all matters referred to in paragraphs 2 and 4 of Article III,* any advantage, favour, privilege or immunity granted by any contracting party to any product originating in or destined for any other country shall be accorded immediately and unconditionally to the like product originating in or destined for the territories of all other contracting parties.

2. The provisions of paragraph 1 of this Article shall not require the elimination of any preferences in respect of import duties or charges which do not exceed the levels provided for in paragraph 4 of this Article and which fall within the following descriptions:

(a) Preferences in force exclusively between two or more of the territories listed in Annex A, subject to the conditions set forth therein;

(b) Preferences in force exclusively between two or more territories which on July 1, 1939, were connected by common sovereignty or relations of protection or suzerainty and which are listed in Annexes B, C and D, Subject to the conditions set forth therein;

(c) Preferences in force exclusively between the United States of America and the Republic of Cuba;

(d) Preferences in force exclusively between neighbouring countries listed in Annexes E and F.

3. The provisions of paragraph 1 shall not apply to preferences between the countries formerly a part of the Ottoman Empire and detached from it on July 24, 1923, provided such preferences are approved under paragraph 5# of Article XXV, which shall be applied in this respect in the light of paragraph 1 of Article XXIX.

4. The margin of preference* on any product in respect of which a preference is permitted under paragraph 2 of this Article but is not specifically set forth as a maximum margin of preference in the appropriate Schedule annexed to this Agreement shall not exceed:

(a) in respect of duties or charges on any product described in such Schedule, the difference between the most-favoured-nation and preferential rates provided for therein; if no preferential rate is provided for, the preferential rate shall for the purposes of this paragraph be taken to be that in force on April 10, 1947, and, if no most-favoured-nation rate is provided for, the margin shall not exceed the difference between the most-favoured-nation and preferential rates existing on April 10, 1947;

(b) in respect of duties or charges on any product not described in the appropriate Schedule, the difference between the most-favoured-nation and preferential rates existing on April 10, 1947.

In the case of the contracting parties named in Annex G, the date of April 10, 1947, referred to in sub-paragraphs (a) and (b) of this paragraph shall be replaced by the respective dates set forth in that Annex.

* *Source: General Agreement on Tariffs and Trade.* Basic Instruments and Selected Documents, Vol. IV, 1969.

The authentic text erroneously reads "sub-paragraph 5(a)".7

APPENDIX II

General Agreement on Tariffs and Trade

Article XVIII*

Governmental Assistance to Economic Development

1. The contracting parties recognize that the attainment of the objective of this Agreement will be facilitated by the progressive development of their economies, particularly of those contracting parties the economies of which can only support low standards of living* and are in the early stages of development.*

2. The contracting parties recognize further that it may be necessary for those contracting parties, in order to implement programmes and policies of economic development designed to raise the general standard of living of their people, to take protective or other measures affecting imports, and that such measures are justified in so far as they facilitate the attainment of the objectives of this Agreement. They agree, therefore, that those contracting parties should enjoy additional facilities to enable them (a) to maintain sufficient flexibility in their tariff structure to be able to grant to tariff protection required for the establishment of a particular industry* and (b) to apply quantitative restrictions for balance of payments purposes in a manner which takes full account of the continued high level of demand for imports likely to be generated by their programmes of economic development.

3. The contracting parties recognize finally that, with those additional facilities which are provided for in Sections A and B of this Article, the provisions of this Agreement would normally be sufficient to enable contracting parties to meet the requirements of their economic development. They agree, however, that there may be circumstances where no measure consistent with those provisions is practicable to

permit a contracting party in the process of economic development to grant the governmental assistance required to promote the establishment of particular industries* with a view to raising the general standard of living of its people. Special procedures are laid down in Sections C and D of this Article to deal with those cases.

4. (a) Consequently, a contracting party the economy of which can only support low standards of living* and is in the early stages of development* shall be free to deviate temporarily from the provisions of the other Articles of this Agreement, as provided in Sections A, B and C of this Article.

(b) A contracting party the economy of which is in the process of development, but which does not come within the scope of sub-paragraph (a) above, may submit applications to the CONTRACTING PARTIES under Section D of this Article.

5. The contracting parties recognize that the export earnings of contracting parties, the economies of which are of the type described in paragraph 4(a) and (b) above and which depend on exports of a small number of primary commodities, may be seriously reduced by a decline in the sale of such commodities. Accordingly, when the exports of primary commodities by such a contracting party are seriously affected by measures taken by another contracting party, it may have resort to the consultation provisions of Article XXII of this Agreement.

6. The CONTRACTING PARTIES shall review annually all measures applied pursuant to the provisions of Sections C and D of this Article.

Section A

7. (a) If a contracting party coming within the scope of paragraph 4(a) of this Article considers it desirable, in order to promote the establishment of a particular industry* with a view to raising the general standard of living of its people, to modify or withdraw a concession included in the appropriate Schedule annexed to this Agreement, it shall notify the CONTRACTING PARTIES to this effect and enter into negotiations with any contracting party with which such concession was initially negotiated, and with any other contracting party determined by the CONTRACTING PARTIES to have a substantial interest therein. If agreement is reached between such contracting parties concerned, they shall be free to modify or withdraw concessions under the appropriate Schedules to this Agreement in order to give effect to such agreement, including any compensatory adjustments involved.

(b) If agreement is not reached within sixty days after the notification provided for in sub-paragraph (a) above, the contracting party which proposes to modify or withdraw the concession may refer the matter to the CONTRACTING PARTIES, which shall promptly examine it. If they find that the contracting party which proposes to modify or withdraw the concession has made every effort to reach an agreement and that the compensatory adjustment offered by it is adequate, that contracting party shall be free to modify or withdraw the concession if, at the same time, it gives effect to the compensatory adjustment. If the CONTRACTING PARTIES do not find that the compensation offered by a contracting party proposing to modify or withdraw the concession is adequate, but find that it has made every reasonable effort to offer adequate compensation, that contracting party shall be free to proceed with such modification or withdrawal. If such action is taken, any other contracting party referred to in sub-paragraph (a) above shall be free to modify or withdraw substantially equivalent concessions initially negotiated with the contracting party which has taken the action*.

Section B

8. The contracting parties recognize that contracting parties coming within the scope of paragraph 4(a) of this Article tend, when they are in rapid process of development, to experience balance of payments difficulties arising mainly from efforts to expand their internal markets as well as from the instability in their terms of trade.

9. In order to safeguard its external financial position and to ensure a level of reserves adequate for the implementation of its programme of economic development, a contracting party coming within the scope of paragraph 4(a) of this Article may, subject to the provisions of paragraphs 10 to 12, control the general level of its imports by restricting the quantity or value of merchandise permitted to be imported; *Provided* that the import restrictions instituted, maintained or intensified shall not exceed those necessary:

(a) to forestall the threat of, or to stop, a serious decline in its monetary reserves, or
(b) in the case of a contracting party with inadequate monetary reserves, to achieve a reasonable rate of increase in its reserves.

Due regard shall be paid in either case to any special factors which may be affecting the reserves of the contracting party or its need for reserves, including, where special external credits or other resources are available to it, the need to provide for the appropriate use of such credits or resources.

10. In applying these restrictions, the contracting party may determine their incidence on imports of different products or classes of products in such a way as to give priority to the importation of those products which are more essential in the light of its policy of economic development; *Provided* that the restrictions are so applied as to avoid unnecessary damage to the commercial or economic interests of any other contracting party and not to prevent unreasonably the importation of any description of goods in minimum commercial quantities the exclusion of which would impair regular channels of trade; and *Provided* further that the restrictions are not so applied as to prevent the importation of commercial sample or to prevent compliance with patent,

trade mark, copyright or similar procedures.

11. In carrying out its domestic policies, the contracting party concerned shall pay due regard to the need for restoring equilibrium in its balance of payments on a sound and lasting basis and to the desirability of assuring an economic employment of productive resources. It shall progressively relax any restriction applied under this Section as conditions improve, maintaining them only to the extent necessary under the terms of paragraph 9 of this Article and shall eliminate them when conditions no longer justify such maintenance; *Provided* that no contracting party shall be required to withdraw or modify restrictions on the ground that a change in its development policy would render unnecessary the restrictions which it is applying under this Section.*

12. (a) Any contracting party applying new restrictions or raising the general level of its existing restrictions by a substantial intensification of the measures applied under this Section, shall immediately after instituting or intensifying such restrictions (or, in circumstances in which prior consultation is practicable, before doing so) consult with the CONTRACTING PARTIES as to the nature of its balance of payments difficulties, alternative corrective measures which may be available, and the possible effect of the restrictions on the economies of other contracting parties.

(b) On a date to be determined by them*, the CONTRACTING PARTIES shall review all restrictions still applied under this Section on that date. Beginning two years after that date, contracting parties applying restrictions under this Section shall enter into consultations of the type provided for in sub-paragraph (a) above with the CONTRACTING PARTIES at intervals of approximately, but not less than, two years according to a programme to be drawn up each year by the CONTRACTING PARTIES; *Provided* that no consultation under this sub-paragraph shall take place within two years after the conclusion of a consultation of a general nature under any other provision of this paragraph.

(c) (i) If, in the course of consultations with a contracting party under sub-paragraph (a) or (b) of this paragraph, the CONTRACTING PARTIES find that the restrictions are not consistent with the provisions of this Section or with those of Article XIII (subject to the provisions of Article XIV), they shall indicate the nature of the inconsistency and may advise that the restrictions by suitably modified.

(ii) If, however, as a result of the consultations, the CONTRACTING PARTIES determine that the restrictions are being applied in a manner involving an inconsistency of a serious nature with the provisions of this Section or with those of Article XIII (subject to the provisions of Article XIV) and that damage to the trade of any contracting party is caused or threatened thereby, they shall so inform the contracting party applying the restrictions and shall make appropriate recommendations for securing conformity with such provisions within a specified period. If such contracting party does not comply with these recommendations within the specified period, the CONTRACTING PARTIES may release any contracting party the trade of which is adversely affected by the restrictions from such obligations under this Agreement towards the contracting party applying the restrictions as they determine to be appropriate in the circumstances.

(d) The CONTRACTING PARTIES shall invite any contracting party which is applying restrictions under this Section to enter into consultations with them at the request of any contracting party which can establish a *prima facie* case that the restrictions are inconsistent with the provisions of this Section or with those of Article XIII (subject to the provisions of Article XIV) and that its trade is adversely affected thereby. However, no such invitation shall be issued unless the CONTRACTING PARTIES have ascertained that direct discussions between the contracting parties concerned have not been successful. If, as a result of the consultations with the CONTRACTING PARTIES no agreement is reached and they determine that the restrictions are being applied inconsistently with such provisions, and that damage to the trade of the contracting party initiating the procedure is caused or threatened thereby, they shall recommend the withdrawal or modification of the restrictions. If the restrictions are not withdrawn or modified within such time as the CONTRACTING PARTIES may prescribe, they may release the contracting party initiating the procedure from such obligations under this Agreement towards the contracting party applying the restrictions as they determine to be appropriate in the circumstances.

(e) If a contracting party against which action has been taken in accordance with the last sentence of sub-paragraph (c)(ii) or (d) of this paragraph, finds that the release of obligations authorized by the CONTRACTING PARTIES adversely affects the operation of its programme and policy of economic development, it shall be free, not later than sixty days after such action is taken, to give written notice to the Executive Secretary[1] to the CONTRACTING PARTIES of its intention to withdraw from this Agreement and such withdrawal shall take effect on the sixtieth day following the day on which the notice is received by him.

(f) In proceeding under this paragraph, the CONTRACTING PARTIES have due regard to the factors referred to in paragraph 2 of this Article. Determinations under this paragraph shall be rendered expeditiously and, if possible, within sixty days of the initiation of the consultations.

Source: *Ibid*

APPENDIX III

General Agreement on Tariffs and Trade

TRADE AND DEVELOPMENT

Article XXXVI

Principles and Objectives

1.* The contracting parties,

(a) recalling that the basic objectives of this Agreement include the raising of standards of living and the progressive development of the economies of all contracting parties, and considering that the attainment of these objectives is particularly urgent for less-developed contracting parties;

(b) considering that export earnings of the less-developed contracting parties can play a vital part in their economic development and that the extent of this contribution depends on the prices paid by the less-developed contracting parties for essential imports, the volume of their exports, and the prices received for these exports;

(c) noting, that there is a wide gap between standards of living in less-developed countries and in other countries;

(d) recognizing that individual and joint action is essential to further the development of the economies of less-developed contracting parties and to bring about a rapid advance in the standards of living in these countries;

(e) recognizing that international trade as a means of achieving economic and social advancement should be governed by such rules and procedures – and measures in conformity with such rules and procedures – as are consistent with the objectives set forth in this Article;

(f) noting that the CONTRACTING PARTIES may enable less-developed contracting parties to use special measures to promote their trade and development;

agree as follows.

2. There is need for a rapid an sustained expansion of the export earnings of the less-developed contracting parties.

3. There is need for positive efforts designed to ensure that less-developed contracting parties secure a share in the growth in international trade commensurate with the needs of their economic development.

4. Given the continued dependence of many less-developed contracting parties on the exportation of a limited range of primary products*, there is need to provide in the largest possible measure more favourable and acceptable conditions of access to world markets for these products and wherever appropriate to devise measures designed to stabilize and improve conditions of world markets in these products, including in particular measures designed to attain stable, equitable and remunerative prices, thus permitting an expansion of world trade and demand and a dynamic and steady growth of the real export earnings of these countries so as to provide them with expanding resources for their economic development.

5. The rapid expansion of the economies of the less-developed contracting parties will be facilitated by a diversification* of the structure of their economies and the avoidance of an excessive dependence on the export of primary products. There is, therefore, need for increased access in the largest possible measure to markets under favourable conditions for processed and manufactured products currently or potentially of particular export interest to less-developed contracting parties.

6. Because of the chronic deficiency in the export proceeds and other foreign exchange earnings of less-developed contracting parties, there are important inter-relationships between trade and financial assistance to development. There is, therefore, need for close and continuing collaboration between the CONTRACTING PARTIES and the international lending agencies so that they can contribute most effectively to alleviating the burdens these less-developed contracting parties assume in the interest of their economic development.

7. There is need for appropriate collaboration between the CONTRACTING PARTIES, other inter-governmental bodies and the organs and agencies of the United Nations system, whose activities relate to the trade and economic development of less-developed countries.

8. The developed contracting parties do not expect reciprocity for commitments made by them in trade negotiations to reduce or remove tariffs and other barriers to the trade of less-developed contracting

parties.*

9. The adoption of measures to give effect to these principles and objectives shall be a matter of conscious and purposeful effort on the part of the contracting parties both individually and jointly.

Article XXXVII

Commitments

1. The developed contracting parties shall to the fullest extent possible — that is, except when compelling reasons, which may include legal reasons, make it impossible — give effect to the following provisions:

(a) accord high priority to the reduction and elimination of barriers to products currently or potentially of particular export interest to less-developed contracting parties, including customs duties and other restrictions which differentiate unreasonably between such products in their primary and in their processed forms*;

(b) refrain from introducing, or increasing the incidence of, customs duties or non-tariff import barriers on products currently or potentially of particular export interest to less-developed contracting parties; and

(c) (i) refrain from imposing new fiscal measures, and

(ii) in any adjustments of fiscal policy accord high priority to the reduction and elimination of fiscal measures,

which would hamper, or which hamper, significantly the growth of consumption of primary products, in raw or processed from, wholly or mainly produced in the territories of less-developed contracting parties, and which are applied specifically to those products.

2. (a) Whenever it is considered that effect is not being given to any of the provisions of sub-paragraph (a), (b) or (c) of paragraph 1, the matter shall be reported to the *Contracting Parties* either by the contracting party not so giving effect to the relevant provisions or by any other interested contracting party.

(b) (i) The *Contracting Parties* shall, if requested so to do by any interested contracting party, and without prejudice to any bilateral consultations that may be undertaken, consult with the contracting party concerned and all interested contracting parties with respect to the matter with a view to reaching solutions satisfactory to all contracting parties concerned in order to further the objectives set forth in Article XXXVI. In the course of these consultations, the reasons given in cases where effect was not being given to the provisions of sub-paragraph (a), (b) of (c) or paragraph 1 shall be examined.

(ii) As the implementation of the provisions of sub-paragraph (a), (b) or (c) of paragraph 1 by individual contracting parties may in some cases be more readily achieved where action is taken jointly with other developed contracting parties, such consultation might, where appropriate, be directed towards this end.

(iii) The consultations by the CONTRACTING PARTIES might also, in appropriate cases, be directed towards agreement on joint action designed to further the objectives of this Agreement as envisaged in paragraph 1 of Article XXV.

3. The developed contracting parties shall:

(a) make every effort, in cases where a government directly or indirectly determines the resale price of products wholly or mainly produced in the territories of less-developed contracting parties, to maintain trade margins at equitable levels;

(b) give active consideration to the adoption of other measures* designed to provide greater scope for the development of imports from less-developed contracting parties and collaborate in appropriate international action to this end;

(c) have special regard to the trade interests of less-developed contracting parties when considering the application of other measures permitted under this Agreement to meet particular problems and explore all possibilities of constructive remedies before applying such measures where they would affect essential interests of those contracting parties.

4. Less-developed contracting parties agree to take appropriate action in implementation of the provisions of Part IV for the benefit of the trade of other less-developed contracting parties, in so far as such action is consistent with their individual present and future development, financial and trade needs taking into account past trade developments as well as the trade interests of less-developed contracting parties as a whole.

5. In the implementation of the commitments set forth in paragraphs 1 to 4 each contracting party shall afford to any other interested contracting party or contracting parties full and prompt opportunity for consultations under the normal procedures of this Agreement with respect to any matter or difficulty which may arise.

Article XXXVII

Joint Action

1. The contracting parties shall collaborate jointly, within the framework of this Agreement and elsewhere, as appropriate, to further the objectives set forth in Article XXXVI.

2. In particular, the CONTRACTING PARTIES shall:

(a) where appropriate, take action, including action through international arrangements, to provide improved and acceptable conditions of access to world markets for primary products of particular interest to less-developed contracting parties and to devise measures designed to stabilize and improve conditions of world markets in these products including measures designed to attain stable, equitable and remunerative prices for exports of such products;

(b) seek appropriate collaboration in matters of trade and development policy with the United Nations and its organs and agencies, including any institutions that may be created on the basis of recommendations by the United Nations Conference of Trade and Development;

(c) collaborate in analysing the development plans and policies of individual less-developed contracting parties and in examining trade and aid relationships with a view to devising concrete measures to promote the development of export potential and to facilitate access to export markets for the products of the industries thus developed and, in this connexion, seek appropriate collaboration with governments and international organizations, and in particular with organizations having competence in relation to financial assistance for economic development, in systematic studies of trade and aid relationships in individual less-developed contracting parties aimed at obtaining a clear analysis of export potential, market prospects and any further action that may be required;

(d) keep under continuous review the development of world trade with special reference to the rate of growth of the trade of less-developed contracting parties and make such recommendations to contracting parties as may, in the circumstances, be deemed appropriate;

(e) collaborate in seeking feasible methods to expand trade for the purpose of economic development, through international harmonization and adjustment of national policies and regulations, through technical and commercial standards affecting production, transportation and marketing, and through export promotion by the establishment of facilities for the increased flow of trade information and the development of market research; and

(f) establish such institutional arrangements as may be necessary to further the objective set forth in Article XXXVI and to give effect to the provisions of this Part.

Source: *Ibid*

* "For the convenience of the reader, asterisks mark the portion of the text which should be read in conjunction with notes and supplementary provisions in Annex I to the Agreement" GATT Articles *Preface*. Interested readers may see the relevant annexes contained in GATT, *Basic Instruments and Selected Documents, Vol. IV*, 1969.

APPENDIX IV

Programme of Action on the Establishment of a New International Economic Order

(Vide Resolution No. 3202(S-VI) adopted by the UN General Assembly on 1st May, 1974)

RELEVANT PORTIONS

Introduction

1. In view of the continuing severe economic imbalance in the relations between developed and developing countries, and in the context of the constant and continuing aggravation of the imbalance of the economies of the developing countries and the consequent need for the mitigation of their current economic difficulties, urgent and effective measures need to be taken by the international community to assist the developing countries, while devoting particular attention to the least developed, land-locked and island developing countries and those developing countries most seriously affected by economic crises and natural calamities leasing to serious retardation of development processes.

2. With a view to ensuring the application of the Declaration on the Establishment of a New International Economic Order[1], it will be necessary to adopt and implement within a specified period of programme of action of unprecedented scope and to bring about maximum economic cooperation and understanding among all State, particularly between developed and developing countries, based on the principles of dignity and sovereign equality.

1. General Assembly resolution 3201 (S-VI).

I FUNDAMENTAL PROBLEMS OF RAW MATERIALS AND PRIMARY COMMODITIES AS RELATED TO TRADE AND DEVELOPMENT

1. *Raw Materials*

All efforts should be made:

(a) To put an end to all forms of foreign occupation, racial discrimination, apartheid, colonial, neo-colonial and alien domination and exploitation through the exercise of permanent sovereignty over natural resources;

(b) To take measures for the recovery, exploitation, development, marketing and distribution of natural resources, particularly of developing countries, to serve their national interests, to promote collective self-reliance among them and to strengthen mutually beneficial international economic co-operation with a view to bringing about the accelerated development of developing countries.

2. *Food*

All efforts should be made:

(a) To promote exports of food products of developing countries through just and equitable arrangements, inter alia, by the progressive elimination of such protective and other measures as constitute unfair competition.

3. *General Trade*

All efforts should be made:

(a) To take the following measures for the amelioration of terms of trade of developing countries and concrete steps to eliminate chronic trade deficits of developing countries:

(i) Fulfilment of relevant commitments already undertaken in the United Nations Conference on Trade and Development and in the International Development Strategy for the Second United Nations Development Decade;[2]

(ii) Improved access to markets in developed countries through the progressive removal of tariff and non-tariff barriers and of restrictive business practices;

(iii) Expeditious formulation of commodity agreements where

2. General Assembly Resolution 2626 (XXV).

appropriate, in order to regulate as necessary and to stabilise the world markets for raw materials and primary commodities;

(iv) Preparation of an over-all integrated programme, setting out guidelines and taking into account the current work in this field, for a comprehensive range of commodities of export interest to developing countries;

(v) Where products of developing countries compete with the domestic production in developed countries, each developed country should facilitate the expansion of imports from developing countries and provide a fair and reasonable opportunity to the developing countries to share in the growth of the market;

(vi) When the importing developed countries derive receipts from customs duties, taxes and other protective measures applied to imports of these products, consideration should be given to the claim of the developing countries that these receipts should be reimbursed in full to the exporting developing countries or devoted to providing additional resources to meet their development needs;

(vii) Developed countries should make appropriate adjustments in their economies so as to facilitate the expansion and diversification of imports from developing countries and thereby permit a rational, just and equitable international division of labour;

(viii) Setting up general principles for pricing policy for exports of commodities of developing countries with a view to rectifying and achieving satisfactory terms of trade for them;

(ix) Until satisfactory terms of trade are achieved for all developing countries, consideration should be given to alternative means, including improved compensatory financing schemes for meeting the development needs of the developing countries concerned;

(x) Implementation, improvement and enlargement of the generalised system of preferences for exports of agricultural primary commodities, manufactures and semi-manufactures from developing to developed countries and consideration of its extension to commodities, including those which are processed or semi-processed; developing countries which are or will be sharing their existing tariff advantages in some developed countries as the result of the introduction and eventual enlargement of the generalized system of preferences should, as a matter of urgency, be granted new openings in the markets of other developed countries which should offer them export opportunities that at least compensate for the sharing of those advantages;

(xi) The setting up of buffer stocks within the framework of commodity arrangements and their financing by international financial institutions, wherever necessary, by the developed countries and, when they are able to do so, by the developing countries, with the aim of favouring the producer developing and consumer developing countries and of contributing to the expansion of world trade as a whole;

(xii) In cases where natural materials can satisfy the requirements of the market, new investment for the expansion of the capacity to produce synthetic materials and substitutes should not be made.

(b) To be guided by the principles of non-reciprocity and preferential treatment of developing countries in multilateral trade negotiations between developed and developing countries, and to seek sustained and additional benefits for the international trade of developing countries, so as to achieve substantial increase in their foreign exchange earnings, diversification of their exports and acceleration of the rate of their economic growth.

VII PROMOTION OF CO-OPERATION AMONG DEVELOPING COUNTRIES

1. Collective self-reliance and growing co-operation among developing countries will further strengthen their role in the new international economic order. Developing countries, with a view to expanding co-operation at the regional, sub-regional and inter-regional levels, should take further steps, inter alia;

(a) To support the establishment and/or improvement of an appropriate mechanism to defend the prices of their exportable commodities and to improve access to an stabilize markets for them. In this context the increasingly effective mobilization by the whole group of oil-exporting countries of their natural resources for the benefit of their economic development is to be welcomed. At the same time there is the paramount need for co-operation among the developing countries in evolving urgently and in a spirit of solidarity all possible means to assist developing countries to cope with the immediate problems resulting from this legitimate and perfectly justified action. The measures already taken in this regard are a positive indication of the evolving co-operation between developing countries;

(b) To protect their inalienable right to permanent sovereignty over their natural resources;

(c) To promote, establish or strengthen economic integration at the regional and subregional levels;

(d) To increase considerably their imports from other developing countries;

(e) To ensure that no developing country accords to imports from developed countries more favourable treatment than that accorded to imports from developing countries. Taking into account the existing international agreements, current limitations and possibilities and also their future evolution, preferential treatment should be given to the procurement of import requirements from other developing countries. Wherever possible, preferential treatment should be given to imports from developing countries and the exports of those countries;

(f) To promote close co-operation in the fields of finance, credit relations and monetary issues, including the development of credit relations on a preferential basis and on favourable terms;

(g) To strengthen efforts which are already being made by developing countries to utilize available financial resources for financing development in the developing countries through investment, financing of export-oriented and emergency projects and other long-term assistance.

(h) To promote and establish effective instruments of co-operation in the fields of industry, science and technology, transport, shipping and mass communication media.

2. Developed countries should support initiatives in the regional, subregional and inter-regional co-operation of developing countries through the extension of financial and technical assistance by more effective and concrete actions, particularly in the field of commercial policy.

Source: *UN Year Book*

APPENDIX V

Basic Principles and Procedures Governing an Agreement on the General System of Preferences

Draft decision submitted by: Afghanistan, Algeria, Argentina, Barbados, Bolivia, Brazil, Burma, Burundi, Cambodia, Cameroon, Central African Republic, Ceylon, Chad, Chile, Colombia, Congo (Brazzaville), Congo (Democratic Republic of), Costa Rica, Cyprus, Dominican Republic, Ecuador, Ethiopia, Gabon, Gambia, Ghana, Guatemala, Guinea, Guyana Honduras, India, Indonesia, Iran, Iraq, Ivory Cost, Jamaica, Jordan, Kenya, Kuwait, Laos, Lebanon, Lesotho, Liberia, Libya, Madagascar, Malaysia, Malawi, Mali, Mauritania, Mexico, Morocco, Nepal, Nicaragua, Niger, Nigeria, Pakistan, Peru, Philippines, Republic of Korea, Republic of Vietnam, Rwanda, Saudi Arabia, Senegal, Sierra Leone, Singapore, Somalia, Southern Yemen, Sudan, Syria, Thailand, Togo, Trinidad and Tobago, Tunisia, Uganda, United Arab Republic, United Republic of Tanzania, Upper Volta, Uruguay, Venezuela, Yemen, Yugoslavia and Zambia (TD/II/C.2 L.5)

Article 1

The United Nations Conference on Trade and Development decides that all developed countries shall establish a general non-discriminatory and non-reciprocal system for preferences providing for unrestricted duty-free entry of all manufactures and semi-manufactures, including processed and semi-processed agricultural and other primary products in favour of all developing countries to increase their export earnings and to accelerate the rate of their economic growth. To this end an international agreement on a general system of preferences on a non-discriminatory and non-reciprocal basis will be concluded and will be applied not later than 1 January 1970.

Article 2

The system of preferences under article 1 shall provide for unrestricted and duty-free access to the markets of all developed countries for all manufactures and semi-manufactures, including agricultural and other primary products in processed and semi-processed form from all developing countries*.

Article 3

All countries of the Group of 77 shall be considered as developing countries entitled to benefit from the general system of preferences under article 1.

Article 4

On grounds of overriding national economic interests, each developed country may, subject to prior international consultation and justification procedure, establish the lists of temporary exceptions of:

(a) Products to which initially substantially reduced rates of duty below the most-favoured-nation level may be applied instead of duty-free entry.
(b) Products to which preferential tariff treatment may be exceptionally and temporarily withheld completely.

Article 5

As a special measure to assist the least developed among the developing countries to receive full benefits of the system, without discriminating among developing countries, and subject to the international consultations and justification procedure envisaged in article 4, the categories of export products of the least developed among the developing countries must not be included in the exceptions lists under article 4(b).

Article 6

Exceptions under article 4 above should be kept to the barest minimum of cases and should relate only to the specific products and not to broad categories so as not to prevent a reasonable growth in the actual export earnings of the developing countries. These exceptions should be subject to periodic reviews for the purpose of reducing and eliminating them.

* In order to identify the products, account will be taken of the appropriate technical documentation, including at least the Brussels Tariff Nomenclature and TD/B/C.2/3.

Article 7

On the basis of internationally agreed objective criteria, a developed country may, after prior international consultation and approval, temporarily invoke the escape clause on specific products of developing countries in case imports from these countries under the preferential regime are held directly responsible for causing serious injury to its domestic industry. In no case shall the preferential entry of these products be restricted below the level reached in the year preceding that in which the escape clause in invoked. In establishing objective economic criteria, the interests of the developing and the developed countries will be taken into account equally.

Article 8

The escape clause action, envisaged in article 7 above, shall not apply to imports of the less competitive products from the less advanced countries.

Article 9

In order to make the system of preferences fully effective in terms of the expansion of the developing countries' export earning, the developed countries shall undertake anticipatory as well as subsequent domestic structural re-adjustment, so as to bring about the expeditious reduction of exceptions lists and to make the escape clause actions either unnecessary or temporary in nature.

Article 10

The developed countries undertake to remove measures which may have the effect of nullifying or reducing the value of preferential treatment envisaged under this agreement to any developing country and to refrain from imposing any new such measures.

Article 11

In order to achieve the objective of the general preferential system, the arrangement should last long enough to enable all developing countries to benefit from it. Initially, the agreement should last for twenty years and should be reviewed towards the end of this initial period. The objectives of this review may, *inter alia*, include the following:

(a) Whether all developing countries are enjoying adequate benefits;
(b) Whether the existing beneficiaries of existing preferences are receiving equivalent advantages;
(c) Whether the system is to be extended or modified; and
(d) Whether some products of developing countries or industries

which have reached an adequate degree of international competitiveness should be excluded.

In any event the preferential treatment should not thereafter be abruptly terminated.

Article 12

The agreement under article 1 should provide for periodic triennial international reviews of the functioning of the system of preferences with a view to assessing the results achieved and to introducing necessary improvement, and particularly to make it possible for the least advanced among the developing countries which have no satisfactorily benefited from the system to obtain further benefits from it.

Article 13

In order to make it possible for the least advanced developing countries to share in the benefits of the preferential system specific commitments should be made by developed countries from the inception of the system to provide, together with the adoption of special commercial policy measures other than those related to conditions of access to their markets, technical and financial and financial assistance through international agencies, as appropriate to the least advanced developing countries in the establishment in their territories of expert-oriented industries geared towards the markets of both the developed and other developing countries.

Article 14

The new system of general preferences should ensure at least equivalent advantages to developing countries enjoying preferences in certain developed countries to enable them to suspend their existing preferences on manufactures and semi-manufactures, including processed and semi-processed agricultural and other primary products. From the beginning, provision should be incorporated in the system of general preferences, for the developed countries to redress any adverse situation which may arise for these developing countries as a consequence of the institution of the general system of preferences.

The body that will be charged with the implementation of the general system of preferences shall, at the end of five years after application of the general system of preferences, examine and review the situation of developing countries now enjoying of the less advantageous system with the more advantageous system without adversely affecting the global export opportunities of any developing country.

If the general system proves detrimental to countries benefiting from special systems, the body given the task of implementing the general system will also have to determine satisfactory compensatory measures to be taken by the developed countries while at the same time the special preferences are progressively eliminated, in order to ensure at least equivalent advantages for the beneficiary countries.

During the same transitional period the present arrangements for certain developed countries that enjoy special preferences for their products in certain developing countries should be brought into line through bilateral consultations or other appropriate procedures, as the case may be, with the new system of preferences under which only the products of all developing countries shall enjoy preferences in the markets of all developed countries. The developed countries shall refrain from taking any retaliatory measures or from demanding any other advantage which would be tantamount to it.

Article 15

A Special Negotiating Committee on Preferences shall be established in order to negotiate the agreement on the system of preferences based on the principles and procedures embodied in this agreement and other arrangements for the functioning of the system of preferences. In addition to the existing membership of the Group on Preferences, the membership of the Special Committee shall be open to those States members of UNCTAD which notify the UNCTAD secretariat not later than 30 April 1968 of their intention of participating in its work.

Article 16

The Special Negotiating Committee for Preferences shall, an order to assure successful conclusion of the Agreement under article 1, in addition to detailed elaboration of the system of preferences under articles 1-14, also solve all problems arising under the general scheme of the system of preferences, such as:

(a) Procedures for the evaluation of any adverse situation which may arise for countries now enjoying preferences and the modalities for redressing any such situation;
(b) The formulation of the basic principles governing rules for determination of origin of goods;
(c) The establishment of agreed time-tables for different preparatory measures, including submission of lists of exceptions;
(d) The laying down of an international justification and consultation procedure, based on objective criteria, for governing recognise to the exceptional measures and safeguard clauses as set forth in this Agreement.

Article 17

The Special Negotiating Committee on Preferences will hold its first meeting on 14 May 1968, and set the time-table for further meetings.

The draft agreement on the system of preferences should be completed not later than the end of October 1968.

The Special Negotiating Committee on Preferences will submit its reports together with the draft agreement to the Trade and Development Board, which will make the final decision on the date for convening a conference of government plenipotentiaries, not latter than January 1969.

Source: UNCTAD, *Manufactures*, Vol. II. (1970)

APPENDIX VI

Generalised System of Preferences as Adopted by UNCTAD-II(1968) MANUFACTURES AND SEMI-MANUFACTURES: PREFERENCES, TARIFF AND NON-TARIFF BARRIERS

21(II) PREFERENTIAL OR FREE ENTRY OF EXPORTS OF MANUFACTURES AND SEMI-MANUFACTURES OF DEVELOPING COUNTRIES TO THE DEVELOPED COUNTRIES*

The United Nations Conference on Trade and Development

Having examined the problems relating to the application of a generalised non-reciprocal, non-discriminatory system of preferences in favour of the developing countries.

Having taken cognizance of the Charter of Algiers (TD/38), the report of the Special Group of the Organisation for Economic Cooperation and Development (OECD) (TD./56) and document TD/II/C.2 L.5 of the Group of "77".

Recognising the progress achieved since the first session of the Conference as reflected in the OECD report which involves a major change in commercial policies as between developed market-economy countries and the developing countries.

Recognising the unanimous agreement in favour of the early establishment of a mutually acceptable system of generalised non-reciprocal and non-discriminatory preferences which would be beneficial to the developing countries.

---

* Adopted by UNCTAD-II

Considering the it was not possible to achieve sufficient progress in respect to some key questions related to this problem.

Convinced of the need for further intensive work so as to elaborate such a system,

1. *Agrees* that the objectives of the generalised non-reciprocal, non-discriminatory system of preferences in favour of the developing countries, including special measures in favour of the least advanced among the developing countries, should be:

   (a) to increase their export earnings;
   (b) to promote their industrialisation;
   (c) to accelerate their rates of economic growth;

2. *Establishes*, to this end, a Special Committee on Preferences, as a subsidiary organ of the Trade and Development Board, to enable all the countries concerned to participate in the necessary consultations. Any member country which is unable to participate in the Special Committee may make its views known to the Secretary-General of UNCTAD who will bring them to the attention of the Special Committee;

3. *Decides* that, for the purpose of the action to be taken in accordance with paragraph 2 above, due account should be taken of the agreements and comments contained in the report of the Second Committee (TD/88 and Corr. 1 to 3);

4. *Requests* that the first meeting of the Special Committee be held in November 1968 to consider the progress made by that time, and further requests that a second meeting be held in the first half of 1969 so that the Committee can draw up its final report to the Board; the aim should be to settle the details of the arrangements in the course of 1969 with a view to seeking legislative authority and the required waiver in GATT as soon as possible thereafter.

5. *Notes* the hope expressed by many countries that the arrangements should enter into effect in early 1970.

Source: H.D. Shourie, UNCTAD-II, *A Step Forward* (IIFT, 1968).

APPENDIX VII

General Agreement on Tariffs and Trade

DIFFERENTIAL AND MORE FAVOURABLE TREATMENT, RECIPROCITY AND FULLER PARTICIPATION OF DEVELOPING COUNTRIES

Decision of 28 November 1979
(L/4903)

Following negotiations within the framework of the Multilateral trade Negotiations, the CONTRACTING PARTIES *decide* as follows:

1. Notwithstanding the provisions of Article I of the General Agreement, contracting parties may accord differential and more favourable treatment to developing countries[1], without according such treatment to other contracting parties.

2. The provisions of paragraph 1 apply to the following:[2]

(a) Preferential tariff treatment accorded by developed contracting parties to products originating in developing countries in accordance with the Generalized System of Preferences,[3]

(b) Differential and more favourable treatment with respect to the provisions of the General Agreement concerning non-tariff measures governed by the provisions of instruments multilaterally negotiated under the auspices of the GATT;

(c) Regional of global arrangements entered into amongst less-developed contracting parties for the mutual reduction or elimination of tariffs and, in accordance with criteria or conditions which may be prescribed by the CONTRACTING PARTIES, for the mutual reduction or elimination of non-tariff measures, on products imported from one another.;

(d) Special treatment of the least developed among the

developing countries in the context of any general or specific measures in favour of developing countries.

3. Any differential and more favourable treatment provided under the clause:

(a) shall be designed to facilitate and promote the trade of developing countries and not to raise barriers to or create undue difficulties for the trade of any other contracting parties;
(b) shall not constitute an impediment to the reduction or elimination of tariffs and other restrictions to trade on a most-favoured-nation basis;
(c) shall in the case of such treatment accorded by developed contracting parties to developing countries be designed and, if necessary, modified, to respond positively to the development, financial and trade needs of developing countries.

4. Any contracting party taking action to introduce an arrangement pursuant to paragraphs 1,2 and 3 above of subsequently taking action to introduce modification or withdrawal of the differential and more favourable treatment so provided shall:[4]

Notification and Consultations

(a) notify the CONTRACTING PARTIES and furnish them with all the information they may deem appropriate relating to such action;
(b) afford adequate opportunity for prompt consultations at the request of any interested contracting party with respect to any difficulty or matter that may arise. The CONTRACTING PARTIES shall, if requested to do so by such contracting party, consult with all contracting parties concerned with respect to the matter with a view to reaching solutions satisfactory to all such contracting parties.

5. The developed countries do not expect reciprocity for commitments made by them in trade negotiations to reduce or remove tariffs and other barriers to the trade of developing countries, i.e., the developed countries do not expect the developing countries, in the course of trade negotiations, to make contributions which are inconsistent with their individual development, financial and trade needs, Developed contracting parties shall therefore not seek, neither shall, less-developed contracting parties be required to make, concessions that are inconsistent with the latters' development, financial and trade needs.

6. Having regard to the special economic difficulties and the particular development, financial and trade needs of the least-developed

countries the developed countries shall exercise the utmost restraint in seeking any concessions or contributions for commitments made by them to reduce or remove tariffs and other barriers to the trade of such countries, and the least-developed countries shall not be expected to make concessions or contributions that are inconsistent with the recognition of their particular situation and problems.

7. The concessions and contributions made and the obligations assumed by developed and less-developed contracting parties under the provisions of the General Agreement should promote the basic objectives of the Agreement, including those embodied in the Preamble and in Article XXXVI. Less-developed contracting parties expect that their capacity to make contributions or negotiated concessions or take other mutually agreed action under the provisions and procedures of the General Agreement (would improve with the progressive development of their economies and improvement in their trade situation and they would accordingly expect to participate more fully in the framework of rights and obligations under the General Agreement.

8. Particular account shall be taken of the serious difficulty of the least-developed countries in making concessions and contributions in view of their special economic situation and their development, financial and trade needs.

9. The contracting parties will collaborate in arrangement for review of the operation of these provisions, bearing in mind the need for individual and joint efforts by contracting parties to meet the development needs of developing countries and the objectives of the General Agreement.

DECLARATION ON TRADE MEASURES TAKEN FOR BALANCE-OF-PAYMENTS PURPOSES

Adopted on 28 November 1979
(L/4904)

The Contracting Parties,

Having regard to the provisions of Articles XII and XVIII:B of the General Agreement;

Recalling the procedures for consultations on balance-of-payments restrictions approved by the Council on 28 April 1970[5] and the procedures for regular consultations on balanced-of-payments restrictions with developing countries approved by the Council on 19 December 1972;[6]

Convinced that restrictive trade measures are in general an inefficient means to maintain or restore balance-of-payments equilibrium;

Noting that restrictive import measures other than quantitative restrictions have been used for balance-of-payments purposes;

Reaffirming that restrictive import measures taken for balance-of-payments purposes should not be taken for the purpose of protecting a particular industry or sector;

Convinced that the contracting parties should endeavour to avoid that restrictive import measures taken for balance-of-payments purposes stimulate new investments that would not be economically viable in the absence of the measures;

Recognizing that the less-developed contracting parties must take into account their individual development, financial and trade situation when implementing restrictive import measures taken for balance-of-payments purposes;

Recognizing that the impact of trade measures taken by developed countries on the economies of developing countries can be serious;

Recognizing that developed contracting parties should avoid the imposition of restrictive trade measures for balance-of-payments purposes to the maximum extent possible.

Agree as follows:

1. The procedures for examination stipulated in Articles XII and XVIII shall apply to all restrictive import measures taken for balance-of-payments purposes. The application of restrictive import measures taken for balance-of-payments purposes shall be subject to the following conditions in addition to those provided for in Articles XII, XIII, XV and XVIII without prejudice to other provisions of the General Agreement:

(a) In applying restrictive import measures contracting parties shall abide by the disciplines provided for in the GATT and give preference to the measures which has the least disruptive effect on trade[7];

(b) The simultaneous application of more than one type of trade measure for this purpose should be avoided.

(c) Whenever practicable, contracting parties shall publicly announce a time schedule for the removal of the measures.

The provisions of this paragraph are not intended to modify substantive provisions of the General Agreement.

2. If, notwithstanding the principles of this Declaration, a developed contracting party is compelled to apply restrictive import measures for balance of-payments purposes, it shall, in determining the incidence of its measures, take into account the export interests of the less-developed contracting parties and may exempt from its measures products of export interest to those contracting parties.

3. Contracting parties shall promptly notify to the GATT the introduction or intensification of all restrictive import measures taken for balance-of-payments purposes. Contracting parties which have

reason to believe that a restrictive import measure applied by another contracting party was taken for balance-of-payments purposes may notify the measure to the GATT or may request the GATT secretariat to seek information on the measure and make it available to all contracting parties if appropriate.

4. All restrictive import measures taken for balance-of-payments purposes shall be subject to consultation in the GATT Committee on Balance-of-Payments Restriction (hereafter referred to as "Committee").

5. The membership of the Committee is open to all contracting parties indicating their wish to serve on it. Efforts shall be made to ensure that the composition of the Committee reflects as far as possible the characteristics of the contracting parties in general in terms of their geographical location, external financial position and stage of economic development.

6. The Committee shall follow the procedures for consultations on balance-of-payments restrictions approved by the Council on 28 April 1970[8] (hereinafter referred to as "full consultation procedures") or the procedures for regular consultation on balance-of-payments restrictions with developing countries approved by the Council on 19 December 1972[9] (hereinafter referred to as "simplified consultation procedures") subject to the provisions set out below.

7. The GATT secretariat, drawing on all appropriate source of information, including the consulting contracting party, shall with a view to facilitating the consultations in the Committee prepare a factual background paper describing the trade aspects of the measures taken, including aspects of particular interest to less-developed contracting parties. The paper shall also cover such other matters as the Committee may determine. The GATT secretariat shall give the consulting contracting party the opportunity to comment on the paper before it is submitted to the Committee.

8. In the case of consultations under Article XVIII:12(b) the Committee shall base its decision on the type of procedure on such factors as the following:

(a) the time elapsed since the last full consultations;

(b) the steps the consulting contracting party has taken in the light of conclusions reached on the occasion of previous consultations;

(c) the changes in the overall level or nature of the trade measures taken for balance-of-payments purposes;

(d) the changes in the balance-of-payments situation or prospects;

(e) whether the balance-of-payments problems are structural or temporary in nature.

9. A less-developed contracting party may at any time request full consultations.

10. The technical assistance services of the GATT secretariat shall, at

the request of a less-developed consulting contracting party, assist in it preparing the documentation for the consultations.

11. The Committee shall report on its consultations to the Council. The reports on full consultations shall indicate:

(a) the Committee's conclusions as well as the facts and reasons on which they are based;

(b) the steps the consulting contracting party has taken in the light of conclusions reached on the occasion of previous consultations;

(c) in the case of less-developed contracting parties, the facts and reasons on which the Committee based its decision on the procedure followed; and

(d) in the case of developed contracting parties, whether alternative economic policy measures are available.

If the Committee finds that the consulting contracting party's measures

(a) are in important respects related to restrictive trade measures maintained by another contracting party[10] or

(b) have a significant adverse impact on the export interests of a less-developed contracting party,

it shall so report to the Council which shall take such further action as it may consider appropriate.

12. In the course of full consultations with a less-developed contracting party the Committee shall, if the consulting contracting party so desires, give particular attention to the possibilities for alleviating and correcting the balance-of-payments problem through measures that contracting parties might take to facilitate an expansion of the export earnings of the consulting contracting party, as provided for in paragraph 3 of the full consultation procedures.

13. If the Committee finds that a restrictive import measures taken by the consulting contracting party for balance-of-payments purpose is inconsistent with the provisions of Article XII, XVIII:B or this Declaration, it shall, in its report to the Council, make such findings as well assist the Council in making appropriate recommendations designed to promote the implementation of Articles XII and XVIII:B and this Declaration. The Council shall keep under surveillance any matter on which it has made recommendations.

SAFEGUARD ACTION FOR DEVELOPMENT PURPOSES

Decision of 28 November 1979
(L/4897)

1. The CONTRACTING PARTIES recognize that the implementation by

less-developed contracting parties of programmes and policies of economic development aimed at raising the standard of living of the people may involve in addition to the establishment of particular industries the development of new or the modification or extension of existing production structures with a view to achieving fuller and more efficient use of resources in accordance with the priorities of their economic development. Accordingly, they agree that a less-developed contracting party may, to achieve these objectives, modify or withdraw concessions included in the appropriate schedules annexed to the General Agreement as provided for in Section A of Article XVIII or, where no measure consistent with the other provisions of the General Agreement is practicable to achieve these objectives, have recourse to Section C of Article XVIII, with the additional flexibility provided for below. In taking such action the less-developed contracting party concerned shall give due regard to the objectives of the General Agreement and to the need to avoid unnecessary damage to the trade of other contracting parties.

2. The Contracting parties recognize further that there may be unusual circumstances where delay in the application of measures which a less-developed contracting party wishes to introduce under Section A or Section C of Article XVIII may give rise to difficulties in the application of its programmes and policies of economic development for the aforesaid purposes. They agree, therefore, that in such circumstances, the less-developed contracting party concerned may deviate from the provisions of Section A and paragraphs 14, 15, 17 and 18 of Section C to the extent necessary for introducing the measures contemplated on a provisional basis immediately after notification.

3. It is understood that all other requirements of the preambular part of Article XVIII and of Sections A and C of that Article, as well as the Notes and Supplementary Provisions set out in Annex I under these Sections will continue to apply to the measures to which this Decision relates.

4. The CONTRACTING PARTIES shall review this Decision in the light of experience with its operation, with a view to determining whether it should be extended, modified or discontinued.

Source: GATT, *Basic Instruments*

NOTES

1. The words "developing countries" as used in this text are to be understood to refer also to developing territories.
2. It would remain open for the CONTRACTING PARTIES to consider on an *an ad hoc* basis under the GATT provisions for joint action any proposals for different and more favourable treatment not falling within the scope of this paragraph.

3. As described in the Decision of the CONTRACTING PARTIES of 25 June 1971, relating to the establishment of "generalized, non-reciprocal and non-discriminatory preferences beneficial to the developing countries" (BISD 18S/24).
4. Nothing in these provisions shall affect the rights of contracting parties under the General Agreement.
5. BISD 18S/48-53.
6. BISD 20S/47-49.
7. It is understood that the less-developed contracting parties must take into account their individual development, financial and trade situation when selecting the particular measure to be applied.
8. BISD 18S/48-53.
9. BISD 20S/47-49.
10. It is noted that such a finding is more likely to be made in the case of recent measures than of measures in effect for some considerable time.
11. As referred to in paragraphs 2, 3, 7, 13 and 22 of Article VIII and in the Note to these paragraphs.

APPENDIX VIII

Ministerial Declaration on the Uruguay Round

Ministers, meeting on the occasion of the Special Session of Contracting Parties at Punta del Este, have decided to launch Multilateral Trade Negotiations (The Uruguay Round). To this end, they have adopted the following Declaration. The Multilateral Trade Negotiations (MTN) will be open to the participation of countries as indicated in Parts I and II of this Declaration. A Trade Negotiations Committee (TNC) is established to carry out the Negotiations. The Trade Negotiations Committee shall hold its first meeting not later than 31 October 1986. It shall meet as appropriate at Ministerial level. The Multilateral Trade Negotiations will be concluded within the four years.

PART I — NEGOTIATIONS ON TRADE IN GOODS

The Contracting Parties meeting at Ministerial level

Determined to halt and reverse protectionism and to remove distortions to trade

Determined also to preserve the basic principles and to further the objectives of the GATT

Determined also to developed a more open, viable and durable multilateral trading system

Convinced that such action would promote growth and development

Mindful of the negative effects of prolonged financial and monetary instability in the world economy, the indebtedness of a large number of less-developed contracting parties, and considering the linkage between trade, money, finance and development

Decide to enter into Multilateral Trade Negotiations on trade in goods within the framework and under the aegis of the General Agreement on Tariffs and Trade.

A. Objectives

Negotiations shall aim to

(i) bring about further liberalization and expansion of world trade to the benefit of all countries, especially less-developed contracting parties, including the improvement of access to markets by the reduction and elimination of tariffs, quantitative restrictions and other non-tariff measurers and obstacles;

(ii) strengthen the role of GATT, improve the multilateral trading system based on the GATT and bring about a wider coverage of world trade under agreed, effective and enforceable multilateral disciplines;

(iii) Increase the responsiveness of the GATT system to the evolving international economic environment, through facilitating necessary structural adjustment, enhancing the relationship of the GATT with the relevant international organizations and taking account of changes in trade patterns and prospects, including the growing importance of trade in high technology products, serious difficulties in commodity markets and the importance of an improved trading environment providing, *inter alia*, for the ability of indebted countries to meet their financial obligations;

(iv) foster concurrent co-operative action at the national and international levels to strengthen the inter-relationship between trade policies and other economic policies affecting growth and development, and to contribute towards continued, effective and determined efforts to improve the functioning of the international monetary system and the flow of financial and real investment resources to developing countries.

B. General Principles Government Negotiations

(i) Negotiations shall be conducted in a transparent manner, and consistent with the objectives and commitments agreed in this Declaration and with the principles of the General Agreement in order to ensure mutual advantage and increased benefits to all participants,

(ii) The launching, the conduct and the implementation of the outcome of the negotiations shall be treated as parts of a single undertaking. However, agreements reached at an early stage may be implemented on a provisional or a definitive basis by agreement prior to the formal conclusion of the negotiations. Early agreements shall be taken into account in assessing the overall balance of the negotiations,

(iii) Balanced concessions should be sought within broad trading areas and subjects to be negotiated in order to avoid unwarranted cross-sectoral demands,

(iv) Contracting Parties agree that the principle of differential and more favourable treatment embodied in Part IV and other relevant provisions of the General Agreement and in the Decision of the Contracting Parties of 28 November 1979 on Differential and More Favourable Treatment, Reciprocity and Fuller Participation of Developing Countries applies to the negotiations. In the implementation of standstill and rollback, particular care should be given to avoiding disruptive effects on the trade less-developed contracting parties,

(v) The developed countries do not expect reciprocity for commitments made by them in trade negotiations to reduce or remove tariffs and other barriers to the trade of developing countries, i.e. the developed countries do not expect the developing countries, in the course of trade negotiations, to make contributions which are inconsistent with their individual development financial and trade needs. Developed contracting parties shall therefore not seek, neither shall less-developed contracting parties be required to make, concessions that are inconsistent with the latter's development, financial and trade needs,

(vi) Less-developed contracting parties expect that their capacity of made contribution or negotiated concessions or take other mutually agreed action or take other mutually agreed action under the provisions and procedures of the General Agreement would improve with the progressive development of their economies and improvement in their trade situation and they would accordingly expect to participate more fully in the framework of rights and obligations under the General Agreement.

(vii) Special attention shall be given to the particular situation and problems of the least-developed countries and to the need to encourage positive measures to facilitate expansion of their trading opportunities. Expeditious implementation of the relevant provisions of the 1982 Ministerial Declaration concerning the least-developed countries shall also be given appropriate attention.

C. Standstill and Rollback

Commencing immediately and continuing until the formal completion of the Negotiations, each participant agrees to apply the following commitments:

Standstill

(i) not to take any trade restrictive or distorting measure inconsistent with the provisions of the General Agreement or the Instruments negotiated within the framework of GATT or under its auspices.

(ii) not to take any trade restrictive or distorting measures in the legitimate exercise of its GATT rights, that would go beyond that which is necessary to remedy specific situations, as provided for in the General Agreement and the Instruments referred to in (i) above;

(iii) not to take any trade measures in such a manner as to improve its negotiating positions.

Rollback

(i) that all trade restrictive or distorting measures inconsistent with the provisions of the General Agreement or Instruments negotiated within the framework of GATT or under its auspices, shall be phased out or brought into conformity within an agreed timeframe not later than by the date of the formal completion of the negotiations, talking into account multilateral agreements, undertakings and understandings, including strengthened rules and disciplines, reached in pursuance of the Objectives of the Negotiations;

(ii) there shall be progressive implementation of this commitment in an equitable basis in consultations among participants concerned, including all affected participants. This commitment shall take account of the concerns expressed by any participant about measures directly affecting its trade interests;

(iii) there shall be no GATT concessions requested for the elimination of these measures.

Surveillance of Standstill and Rollback

Each participant agrees that the implementation of these commitments on standstill and rollback shall be subject to multilateral surveillance so as to ensure that these commitments are being met. The Trade Negotiations Committee will decide on the appropriate mechanisms to carry out the surveillance, including periodic reviews and evaluations. Any participant may bring to the attention of the appropriate surveillance mechanism any action or omissions it believes to be relevant to the fulfilment of these commitments. These notifications should be addressed to the GATT secretariat which may also provide further relevant information.

D. Subjects for Negotiations

Tariffs

Negotiations shall aim, by appropriate methods, to reduce or, as appropriate, eliminate tariffs including the reduction or elimination of high tariffs and tariff escalation. Emphasis shall be given to the expansion of the scope of tariff concessions among all participants.

Non-tariff Measures

Negotiations shall aim to reduce or eliminate non-tariff measures, including quantitative restrictions, without prejudice to any action to be taken in fulfilment of the rollback commitments.

Tropical Products

Negotiations shall aim at the fullest liberalization of trade in tropical products, including in their processed and semi-processed forms and shall cover both tariff and all non-tariff measures affecting trade in these products.

Contracting Parties recognize the importance of trade in tropical product to a large number of less-developed contracting parties and agree that negotiations in this area shall receive special attention, including the timing of the negotiations and the implementation of the results as provided for in B(ii).

Natural Resource-based Products

Negotiations shall aim to achieve the fullest liberalization of trade in natural resource-based products, including in their processed and semi-processed forms. The negotiations shall aim to reduce or eliminate tariff and non-tariff measures, including tariff escalation.

Textiles and Clothing

Negotiations in the area of textiles and clothing shall aim to formulate modalities that would permit the eventual integration of this sector into GATT on the basis of strengthened GATT rules and disciplines, thereby also contributing to the objectives of further liberalization of trade.

Agriculture

Contracting Parties agree that there is an urgent need to bring more discipline and predictability to world agricultural trade by correcting and preventing restrictions and distortions including those related to structural surpluses so as to reduce the uncertainty, imbalance and instability in world agricultural markets. Negotiations shall aim to achieve greater liberalization of trade in agriculture and bring all measures affecting import access and export competition under strengthened and more operationally effective GATT rules and disciplines, taking into account the general principles governing the negotiations, by:

(i) improving market access through, *inter alia*, the reduction of import barriers;

(ii) improving the competitive environment by increasing discipline on the use of all direct and indirect subsidies and other measures affecting directly or indirectly agricultural trade, including the phased reduction of their negative effects and dealing with their causes;

(iii) minimizing the adverse effects that sanitary and phytosanitary regulations and barriers can have on trade in agriculture, taking into account relevant international agreements.

In order to achieve the above objectives, the negotiating group having primary responsibility for all aspects of agriculture will use the Recommendations adopted by the Contracting Parties at their Fortieth Session, which were developed in accordance with the GATT 1982 Ministerial Programme and take account of the approaches suggested in the work of the Committee on Trade in Agriculture without prejudice to other alternatives that might achieve the objectives of the Negotiations.

GATT Articles

Participants shall review existing GATT articles, provisions and disciplines as requested by interested contracting parties, and, as appropriate, undertake negotiations.

Safeguards

(i) A comprehensive agreement on safeguards is of particular importance to the strengthening of the GATT system and to progress of the MTNs.

(ii) The agreement on safeguards:

- shall be based on the basic principles of the General Agreement;
- shall contain, *inter alia*, the following elements: transparency, coverage, objective criteria for action including the concept of serious injury or threat thereof, temporary nature, degressivity and structural adjustment, compensation and realisation notifications, consultation, multilateral surveillance and dispute settlement; and
- shall clarify and reinforce the disciplines of the General Agreement and should apply to all contracting parties.

MTN Agreements and Arrangements

Negotiations shall aim to improve, clarify, or expand, as appropriate, agreements and arrangements negotiated in the Tokyo Round of Multilateral Negotiations.

Subsidies and countervailing measures

Negotiations on subsidies and countervailing measures shall be based on a review of Articles VI and XVI and the MTN agreement on subsidies and countervailing measures with the objective of improving GATT disciplines relating to all subsidies and countervailing measures that effect international trade. A negotiating group will be established to deal with these issues.

Dispute settlement

In order to ensure prompt and effective resolution of disputes to the benefit of all contracting parties, negotiations shall aim to improve and strengthen the rules and the procedures of the dispute settlement process, while recognizing the contribution that would be made by more effective and enforceable GATT rules and disciplines. Negotiations shall include the development of adequate arrangements for overseeing and monitoring of the procedures that would facilitate compliance with adopted recommendations.

Trade-related aspects of intellectual property rights, including trade in counterfeit goods

In order to reduce the distortions and impediments to international trade, and taking into account the need to promote effective and adequate protection of intellectual property rights, and to ensure that measures and procedures to enforce intellectual property rights do not themselves become barriers to legitimate trade, the negotiations shall aim to clarify GATT provisions and elaborate as appropriate new rules and disciplines.

Negotiations shall aim to develop a multilateral framework of principles, rules and disciplines dealing with international trade in counterfeit goods, taking into account work already undertaken in the GATT.

These negotiations shall be without prejudice to other complementary initiatives that may be taken in the World Intellectual Property Organisation and elsewhere to deal with these matters.

Trade-related investment measures

Following an examination of the operation of GATT Articles related to the trade restrictive and distorting effects of investment measures, negotiations should elaborate, as appropriate, further provisions that may be necessary to avoid such adverse effects on trade.

E. Functioning of the GATT System

Negotiations shall aim to develop understandings and arrangements:

(i) to enhance the surveillance in the GATT to enable regular monitoring of trade policies and practices of contracting parties and their impact on the functioning of the multilateral trading system;

(ii) to improve the overall effectiveness and decision-making of the GATT as an institution, including, *inter alia*, through involvement of Ministers,

(iii) to increase the contribution of the GATT to achieving greater coherence in global economic policy-making through strengthening its relationship with other international organisations responsible for monetary and financial matters.

F. Participation

(a) Negotiations will be open to:

(1) all contracting parties,
(2) countries having acceded provisionally,
(3) countries applying the GATT on a *de facto* basis having announced, not later than 30 April 1987, their intention to accede to the GATT and to participate in the negotiations,
(4) countries that have already informed the Contracting Parties, at a regular meeting of the Council of Representatives, of their intention to negotiate the terms of their membership as a contracting party, and
(5) developing countries that have, by 30 April 1987, initiated procedures for accession to the GATT, with the intention of negotiating the terms of their accession during the course of the negotiations.

(b) Participation in negotiations relating to the amendment or application of GATT provisions or the negotiations of new provisions will, however, be open only to contracting parties.

G. Organisation of the Negotiations

A Group of Negotiations on Goods (GNG) is established to carry out the programme of negotiations contained in this Part of the Declaration. The GNG shall, *inter alia*:

(i) elaborate and put into effect detailed trade negotiating plans prior to 19 December 1986;

(ii) designate the appropriate mechanism for surveillance of commitments to standstill and rollback;

(iii) establish negotiating groups as required. Because of the interrelationship of some issues and taking fully into account the general principles governing the negotiations as stated in B(iii) above it is recognized that aspects of one issue may be discussed in more than one negotiating group. Therefore, each negotiating group should as required take into account relevant aspects emerging in other groups;

(iv) also decide upon inclusion of additional subject matters in the negotiations;
(v) co-ordinate the work of the negotiating groups and supervise the progress of the negotiations. As a guideline not more than two negotiating groups should meet at the same time;
(vi) the GNG shall report to the Trade Negotiations Committee.

In order to ensure effective application of differential and more favourable treatment the GNG shall, before the formal completion of the negotiations, conduct an evaluation of the results attained therein in terms of the Objectives and the General Principles Governing Negotiations as set out in the Declaration, taking into account all issues of interest to less-developed contracting parties.

PART II — NEGOTIATIONS ON TRADE IN SERVICES

Ministers also decided, as part of the Multilateral Trade Negotiations, to launch negotiations on trade in services.

Negotiations in this area shall aim to establish a multilateral framework of principles and rules for trade in services, including elaboration of possible disciplines for individual sectors, with a view to expansion of such trade under conditions of transparency and progressive liberalization and as a means of promoting economic growth of all trading partners and the development of developing countries. Such framework shall respect the policy objectives of national laws and regulations applying to services and shall take into account the work of relevant international organizations.

GATT procedures and practices shall apply to these negotiations. A Group on Negotiations on Services is established to deal with these matters. Participation in the negotiations under this Part of the Declaration will be open to the same countries as under Part I. GATT secretariat support will be provided, with technical support from other organizations as decided by the Group of Negotiations on Services.

The Group of Negotiations on Services shall report to the Trade Negotiations Committee.

IMPLEMENTATION OF RESULTS UNDER PARTS I AND II

When the results of the Multilateral Trade Negotiations in all areas have been established, Ministers meeting also on the occasion of a Special Session of Contracting Parties shall decide regarding the international implementation of the respective results.

Source: GATT, Focus, October, 1986.

INDEX